THE RIGHT
WAY TO WIN

Oct. 2001

Jayson,

I saw this book and immediately thought it might be a good one for you. I know it has been a point of struggle - perhaps this will shed some light on being both - athletic & Godly.

Much love always,
Jennifer

THE RIGHT WAY TO WIN

HOW ATHLETES CAN PLACE GOD FIRST IN THEIR HEARTS

Mike Blaylock

MOODY PRESS
CHICAGO

ISBN: 0-8024-8415-8

1 3 5 7 9 10 8 6 4 2

Printed in the United States of America

This book is dedicated
to the two athletes who have most influenced my life:
my daughter, Ashley, and my son, Nathan.
You have provided for me untold joy and inspiration.
I love you guys.

CONTENTS

INTRODUCTION

When asked what he thought about his team's overtime victory over the Texas Longhorns, the Oklahoma Sooners football coach said on national television, "It was Jesus Christ that helped my team to win."

After his crushing TKO win over heavily favored Mike Tyson, Evander Holyfield explained his victory by saying, "My God is the only true God."

In sharp contrast, while voicing the pregame invocation before a recent Dallas Cowboys/Miami Dolphins game, a local Miami minister prayed for a healthy Dan Marino and a Dolphins victory. Marino left the game injured, and the Cowboys won the game.

Athletes today frequently make reference to God or to Jesus Christ after a victory or in a postgame interview. That begins to raise all kinds of questions. What difference does it make to be a Christian and to be an athlete? The Christian athlete who prays more, reads his Bible more, goes to church more, and thinks about God more— is he guaranteed that he'll get more playing time, that he'll be all-American, or even that he'll win the game? What is the relationship between being a Christian and experiencing success as an athlete?

The truth is that God has a specific plan and purpose for the Christian athlete, as you will see. However, it is not always the kind of success printed on the sports page or seen on ESPN. His plan doesn't necessarily lead to the Hall of Fame. His plan is far greater! God's plan for the Christian athlete is for true success—success that is lasting and life changing.

> "For I know the plans that I have for you," declares the Lord, "plans for welfare and not for calamity to give you a future and a hope." (JEREMIAH 29:11)

God's plan for real success comes from within. It begins with your relationship with Him, and it impacts every area of your life. Real success brings victory through setbacks and has far-reaching influence.

Those of you who read this book will do so for different reasons and from different perspectives. Some of you are part-time athletes, some are has-been athletes, and some extremely successful athletes. Some of you are parents of children who participate in sports, and you wonder how to help your child understand how the Bible relates to experiencing success in athletics.

I want to remind you that the principles we are going to cover apply to each situation. The truth is, they are not applicable only to athletes. They are the same principles that apply to having success as a businessman, having success as a parent, having success as a student. In whatever realm or endeavor you undertake, these principles still hold true.

I pray your journey toward success will be one of lasting and eternal significance. I pray it will be a journey that leads to real success, as you learn the only way to win.

1

DISPELLING
THE MYTHS

It was my second year as chaplain for the Kansas City Royals. I had just finished a chapel service for the team when Whitey Herzog, manager of the Royals, pulled me aside. Being somewhat superstitious, he was concerned that we had lost four Sunday games in a row, and he reminded me that I had led the chapel service all four of those Sundays.

He looked me squarely in the eye and said, "If we lose today, you're not coming back down here."

Now, Whitey Herzog was the kind of guy that you never knew if he was just kidding around or was really serious, so I was more than a little concerned about the outcome of the game. I went upstairs, found a seat in the stadium as play began, and pondered the manager's words. Fortunately, I never had to find out about Whitey's intentions, because the Royals won the game 10–1, and I continued to lead weekly chapel services for several more years.

Whitey's superstitious view of the chapel services (I still don't know if he was kidding or serious) is an example of the variety of viewpoints concerning God and sports. There are many myths about the relationship between being a Christian and experiencing success as an athlete, and these have created a great deal of misunderstanding. I have seen athletes attend a pregame chapel service for the single purpose of hoping it would help them break out of a hitting slump. I have seen others make rash promises to God before a competition, believing that would make a difference in the outcome of the game. Other athletes will go through so-called spiritual rituals, trying to gain some kind of an edge over the competition.

What is the relationship between devotion to the Lord and the outcome of the game? Does being a Christian make you a better athlete? If you are more spiritual than your opponent, does God give you extra help in the game? What is myth and what is truth?

MYTH #1: BEING A CHRISTIAN MEANS THE SCORE WILL COME OUT IN YOUR FAVOR.

Shortly before the 1997 Sugar Bowl game between Florida and Florida State, a television show did a segment featuring Christian players from both teams. It was impressive to hear the strong testimonies of athletes and coaches alike from both football teams. There were dynamic Christians on both sides of the field, but only one team, the Florida Gators, came away with the victory that day. If the outcome of a game is affected by the number of committed Christians on the team, then was there a problem with the Christians on the Florida State football team? Were the Florida athletes stronger Christians? Did they pray harder or make a better deal with God? Of course not! Simply being a Christian never guarantees you're going to be on the winning team. God does not have a favorite team.

Former major league manager Sparky Anderson, when asked if the outcome of a game made any difference to God, said, "No, I do not believe God cares about baseball. If he did, you would never have a loser. I am suspicious of guys who think that by attending chapel it is going to help them with their baseball."[1]

Shortly after I graduated from college, I began my coaching career as a high school baseball coach for a Christian school in Tulsa. It was the first year to have a varsity team, and we were small and inexperienced. Despite our size, we played against the other public and private schools in the area. I had two or three boys who could play ball, and the rest of the guys on the team kind of had their hats on sideways and rarely seemed to know what they were doing. It was a long year!

Two of the guys who could play, however, could play with anybody. One was an all-city pitcher, and the other could hit anything thrown his way. He was one of the best hitters I've ever seen. They were two of the best players in the city.

The season progressed, and we wound up playing one of the top-rated teams in the state. The other team came in pretty confident and thought they were going to have an easy time with our new team. My two stars came through, however, and we knocked them off 5–4. The other team wasn't too happy about it and vowed they would have their revenge.

Well, a few weeks passed, and it came time to travel to their turf for a rematch. Just before we were about to leave for that game, I found out that my two stars were ineligible to play because they both had failed a test earlier in the week. So we had to make the trip without our two top players to face a great team that was really fired up to pay us back for beating them.

I decided that my best approach was to pray. I said, "Lord, I need a little help here. I need some words of encouragement. Please give me something I can hang on to today." That morning, I came to Bible reading during my quiet time and got to Psalm 44:11. I opened it up, and there it was: "You give us as sheep to be eaten and have scattered us among the nations." We lost the game 22–2. Thanks for that encouragement, God.

No, being a Christian, being committed to the Lord, reading your Bible, or praying harder never guarantees that you're going to have victory on the field—at least as far as the score is concerned. The difference comes in the character God is able to develop in your life.

MYTH #2: BEING A CHRISTIAN ENSURES THAT YOU'LL BE FREE FROM INJURY.

In a regular season game between the New York Jets and the Kansas City Chiefs, Jets defensive end Dennis Byrd collided with a teammate while attempting to sack the Chiefs' quarterback. The impact shattered his neck and left him paralyzed. Over a period of time and with a great deal of work, Dennis eventually regained the ability to walk, but he will never play football again. He is a devout and dynamic Christian, yet being a Christian did not prevent Dennis Byrd from being injured. But God has used this tragic incident in his life to impact many people with the gospel.

Who can forget seeing San Francisco Giants pitcher Dave Dravecky's arm break as he delivered a pitch shortly after his dramatic comeback from cancer? He would later lose both that arm and his career as a professional baseball player. Once again, Dravecky, a team chapel leader and stand-out Christian, was not exempt from injury because of his personal relationship with God.

The truth of the matter is the Bible tells us that sometimes it is God's will for a Christian to suffer. "For you have been given not only the privilege of trusting in Christ but also the privilege of suffering for him" (Philippians 1:29 NLT). I don't profess to understand all of what that means, but I know from experience that everything does not always turn out the way we want. There are times we must simply trust the Lord. He does understand.

The Christian athlete is never exempt from injury, pain, hurt, or even death. The Christian is only better equipped to handle these difficulties. He has an eternal hope, an unending source of comfort, and a God who has a plan and a purpose bigger than any athletic competition. It is a plan to build real and lasting character.

> Whenever trouble comes your way, let it be an opportunity for joy. For when your faith is tested, your endurance has a chance to grow. So let it grow, for when your endurance is fully developed, you will be strong in character and ready for anything. (JAMES 1:2–4 NLT)

MYTH #3: BEING A CHRISTIAN MEANS THE REFEREE WILL MAKE THE CALL IN YOUR FAVOR.

In 1984, the United States' hopes for an Olympic boxing gold medal in the light heavyweight division rested on the shoulders of a young Christian named Evander Holyfield. His passion for the Lord was evident to every reporter who asked him a question during the games, and his boxing talents were obvious to every analyst who watched him fight. Evander was impressive as he fought his way through the early matches. Finally, only one opponent stood between him and the gold medal match. If he could win this fight, he would be guaranteed at least a silver medal.

Holyfield pummeled the fighter from New Zealand, nearly knocking him down in the first round. In round two, he continued to overwhelm his opponent and then knocked him out in the final seconds of the round. What happened next is still considered one of the most unbelievable calls in sporting history.

The Yugoslavian referee disqualified Holyfield, claiming that he had called for the fighters to break just before the knockout punch was thrown. Even though *both* fighters had thrown punches and no one had heard the referee, the controversial call stood. Sportscaster Howard Cosell would later call it the worse decision he had ever seen. Evander had to settle for the bronze medal, while a fighter from Yugoslavia won the gold by default.[2]

Former major league umpire Ron Luciano speaks about the reality of occasionally missed calls in his book *Strike Two* when he says,

> There are times I found myself standing there with my hands spread out calling a player safe when I just felt like flapping them and taking off. Every umpire occasionally blows a play, and you just hope it doesn't lead to a run, which leads to a victory or loss, which leads to a pennant being won or lost, which leads to twenty thousand to thirty thousand dollars per player in World Series shares.[3]

It doesn't matter if you are a Christian, if you read your Bible every day, or tell every reporter who talks to you that Jesus is Lord; there is no guarantee the referee's calls will go your way. Those calls are outside the realm of your control. They are made by fallible human beings, who sometimes miss a few and in some extreme cases are swayed by other factors. If you remain focused on these things— the things you cannot control—your life will be ruled by circumstances, and you will miss true success.

MYTH #4: BEING A CHRISTIAN MEANS YOU'LL GET MORE PLAYING TIME.

I have a friend who decided to turn down several scholarship offers from smaller schools to play basketball in favor of walking on at a large university. He's a great kid, a very talented athlete, and one of the sharpest Christians I know. I watch his team play ball every time they are on television, and I always see him. He always makes the team highlights on *Sportscenter*. That's, of course, because you can always see him *sitting* in the same spot on the very end of the bench—always.

Being a Christian will not guarantee that you will start on your team—or even get into the game. But being a Christian does mean that God has a specific plan for your life and He is at work in and through you, whether you're in the game or not. It's been my experience that some of the most influential players on a team have often been those who rarely played.

Scott was a wide receiver on the Tulsa University football team when I first met him. An outstanding athlete in high school, he was small and had to work extrahard to play football in a Division 1 program. Injuries kept him on the bench his junior year. He saw some playing time as a senior, but he was never a star. Though he would rather have played far more than he did, there was no one in the four years he was in school who had a bigger impact on the athletic program than Scott.

Often you would pass Scott's room and find several athletes in there with Bibles opened; or you would see him down the hall praying with someone who was struggling with a problem. He took personal interest in the lives of many of the athletes in the dorm. Today many of those same athletes are in full-time ministry and would point to Scott as the reason.

In the long term, who experiences true success? Is it someone who has more playing time or someone who makes a lasting difference in the lives of others? Being a Christian won't get you more playing time, but it does mean God wants to use you whether you are in the game or not. He is at work in your life and will accomplish His plan for you regardless of your playing time.

For we are God's workmanship, created in Christ Jesus to do good works, which God prepared in advance for us to do. (EPHESIANS 2:10 NIV)

MYTH #5: BEING A CHRISTIAN GIVES YOU A PERFORMANCE ADVANTAGE OVER A NON-CHRISTIAN ATHLETE.

Sportswriters love to use the David and Goliath analogy in their headlines. Often a heavily favored team goes down in defeat to the smaller, untouted team. The giant falls to the giant killer—Rocky Balboa defeats Apollo Creed. But David and Goliath were not competing on the athletic field. That was a case of God's chosen people at war against an army that opposed God. There is no athletic comparison.

The truth is that many factors impact the outcome of a competition. For example, injuries or poor performance by a key player can be a huge factor in the downfall of a highly favored team. The bottom line is that an individual athlete can perform only to the absolute best of his ability. Sometimes the other guy is bigger, stronger, and better than you are, and your 100 percent just isn't enough to beat him. I'm sure, no matter how spiritual I may be or how hard I train, if I were to step into the ring with George Foreman, the outcome would be the same every time. I would be lying flat on my back in the middle of the ring, wondering what happened.

I have a friend who has the distinction of having played against the great center Bill Walton in his very first season at UCLA. My friend was the center on the opposing team. He guarded Walton, and he held him to 25 points . . . in the first half. Now, my friend gave his very best, but Walton's best was better. Being a Christian only helps you to give your all. It never guarantees that you will outplay your opponent.

Former major league baseball player Thad Bosley tells of his coming to grips with this truth:

> I've always believed in God, but I had worked out an agreement with Him as far as baseball was concerned. A season earlier I'd been going up to bat against Philly pitcher Larry Anderson. We had been teammates on the 1982 Seattle Mariners and I knew he believed in the same God I did. And as I walked to the plate, it suddenly occurred to me that Larry was out on the mound thinking, all right, God, I want to throw my cut fastball past this guy . . . while I was thinking, okay, God, he's gonna try to throw

that cut fastball past me. . . I had to stop myself from laughing. I knew God wasn't up there saying, sorry, Thad, this time I'm going to make you pop up to third base. I realized that God gave both of us our talent and our ability to use it; the rest was up to us.[4]

Each of us has been blessed with talents and abilities to be used to bring glory to God. Our part is to use them to the very best of our ability. We have no control over the rest. It's that way in the Christian life, whatever you do. The score in the game, the possibility of injury, the referee's calls, your minutes in the game, and your opponent's ability are all things you cannot control.

Face it! There are aspects of your life you cannot do anything about. You have no power over sickness, injury, and the actions and attitudes of other people. As a Christian athlete, you must not allow yourself to be distracted by those things you cannot control. Instead, focus on what you *can* control—your attitudes and your actions. Determine to please your heavenly Father with your performance and your example to those who see. Turn your focus to Him!

Set your mind on the things above, not on the things that are on earth. (COLOSSIANS 3:2)

To Think About

1. What are some ways you have seen the relationship between being a Christian athlete and being successful misunderstood?

2. Why do you think it is easy to be confused about this issue?

3. What difference do you think it really makes to be a Christian and an athlete?

4. List some examples, either from your own life or from those you have observed, about the difference it makes for an athlete to be a Christian.

5. What do you believe should be the measurement of success for a Christian athlete?

6. As an athlete, what can you do to experience success that depends on you and no one else? What can you focus on that will bring true success?

DISCOVERING TRUE SUCCESS

**BUT I KEEP WORKING
TOWARD THAT DAY
WHEN I WILL FINALLY
BE ALL THAT CHRIST
JESUS SAVED ME FOR
AND WANTS ME TO BE.**

(PHILIPPIANS 3:12 NLT)

What is success for an athlete? There are many popular answers to that question. Some would say success is reaching the top of your profession. If that is true, what is left for a twenty-year-old pitcher who wins the MVP in the World Series and leads his team to the championship? Is he doomed to spend the rest of his career clinging to only the memory of a brief moment of success?

Another popular idea relates success to staying at the top of your profession. What then happens to the retiring thirty-four-year-old running back who has been all-pro throughout his career? Is success over for him? As the song says, is that all there is?

Success for some is measured by how well known you become. For some athletes it is getting their name on the wall of the gymnasium, and for others it might be having their own shoe endorsement. However, every athlete understands the downside of this theory— fame is fleeting. It doesn't last. One minute you are the hero and the next the object of boos and criticism. The trip from the cover of *Sports Illustrated* to obscurity can be a very short one. Fame is short-lived. It is never ultimately fulfilling.

Pat Williams is the general manager of the Orlando Magic. He has observed and experienced a great number of accomplishments and successes. He writes about coming to grips with the short-lived satisfaction of these achievements early in his career:

> *The more praise and success came my way, the less satisfied I felt, the more lonely and isolated I seemed to be. I was getting a lot of glory, a lot of ego rushes, a lot of emotional highs—but they were soon over, and the satisfaction they gave me was gone by the next morning. There was a craving inside of me, and I thought I was stuffing all the right things into it— yet the craving refused to be satisfied.[1]*

Still another popular idea of success in athletics is signing a huge multiyear contract. However, the Bible is clear that no long-term happiness comes with riches alone. The book of Proverbs says, "Don't weary yourself trying to get rich. Why waste your time? For riches can disappear as though they had the wings of a bird!" (23:4–5 NLT). Real success is far more than something temporary.

I had just finished doing a chapel service for the California Angels and sat down to visit with a player I had known for several years. Lyman Bostock played outfield for the Angels, and he was telling me about some of the exciting things that were going on in his life. He had recently signed a large (at that time) free-agent contract with the Angels, having previously played for the Twins. He had a new home, a wonderful family, was doing well on the team, and was excited about his relationship with the Lord.

We chatted until he had to go out on the field. That was the last time I saw him. Several days later, while in a car with some relatives, he was accidentally shot to death by a man who was trying to kill someone else. What was the measure of his success at the time of the shotgun blast? Was it determined by his contract, the size of his home, or his batting average? No, all that mattered was his relationship to Jesus Christ and his focus on that relationship. Everything else was meaningless.

Where is your focus? What is important to you? Is it stats? Is it possessions? Is it fame? Is it what other people think about you? Or is it being what God wants you to be?

REAL SUCCESS IS BEING ALL GOD WANTS YOU TO BE

Real Success Prayer #1: *Lord, help me to be everything You want me to be.*

After the death of Moses, God spoke to Joshua, Israel's new leader, and gave him the formula for true success:

> Be strong and very courageous. Obey all the laws Moses gave you. Do not turn away from them, and you will be successful in everything you do. Study this Book of the Law continually. Meditate on it day and night so you may be sure to obey all that is written in it. Only then will you succeed. (JOSHUA 1:7–8 NLT)

God was telling Joshua that if he would simply be all He wanted him to be, then he and the nation of Israel would find success. For the athlete, that success is not measured by the score at the end of the game. It isn't measured by the number of points scored or records set. It is measured by becoming a maximum Christian athlete. It begins by being all God wants you to be as a person. It starts on the inside.

Jeff is a junior linebacker on a Division 1 football team. All year his team has struggled to stay above a .500 record. There is no chance for postseason play, and they are long since out of the conference race. The last several games are all against nationally ranked powerhouse teams. How is it possible for Jeff to experience success the remainder of the season?

The truth is, true success for Jeff is not tied at all to the record of his team or to the outcome of the next two games. Real success is far greater. For him, it is directly related to whether or not he is all God wants him to be. That is where he must be focused.

Dallas Cowboys defensive tackle Chad Hennings writes in his autobiography *It Takes Commitment:*

> *I believe we need to rethink our definition of success. When we observe the people we consider successful versus those we consider unsuccessful, we need to look at things other than money or fame or high position. Instead,*

we should think about how people use what God has given them to be the best they can be. If you do that with your life, no one can ask for anything more.[2]

What does it mean to be all God wants you to be? How do you as a Christian athlete experience real success?

GOD WANTS YOU TO BECOME LIKE JESUS

Real Success Prayer #2: *Make me more like Jesus.*

Romans 8:29 says God wants you to be conformed to the image of His Son. He wants you to be like Christ. So understand this first: You will only find true success as an athlete when you become more like Jesus. That begins by getting to know Him.

When I was in college, I invented a game. It never went video and never had the Milton Bradley stamp of approval on it—but it was a great game. I called it "Leafin'." Here's how it went. My roommate would bury me in the huge collection of leaves right next to the long scenic sidewalk that ran from the dorms to the main campus buildings. He would stand there long enough to tell me who was coming and then he would walk away. I would wait until I heard footsteps next to me, and I would call out the individual's name. After a few seconds of messing with his mind, I would pop up my head and scream. The person would usually run, yell—or, in one isolated case, faint.

The absolutely best people to get in a Leafin' game were some of the ministerial students. After covering me up again, my roommate would tell me the name of the unsuspecting and soon arriving ministerial student. I would again wait until he was close to me and call out his name. Now, the ministerial students would always respond a little differently from the normal victims. They would almost immediately gaze in a heavenly direction. Often they would take off their shoes like Moses before the burning bush. Eventually they would fall on their knees, as if they were on the road to Damascus, believing they now had a strong bond with the apostle Paul.

When I had them where I wanted them, I would then say, "This is the Lord! Go and sell all you have and give it to Mike Blaylock!"

It was a guaranteed winner. I could have financed my entire college education that way.

Now you need to ask yourself an important question: What if God spoke to you? Would you know Him? Would you recognize His voice? Jesus said *His sheep* know *His voice* (John 10:4). How do you get to know His voice?

Impressionists have made a living copying the voices of celebrities. They are able to imitate a voice you and I are familiar with. That's the key—they wouldn't have much success copying voices of people that no one knew. How did the voices of those celebrities become familiar to us? We invested time in getting to know their voices. Perhaps we listened to them on television or in the movies, or maybe we bought their CDs and tapes. In any case, whether deliberately or unintentionally, we spent time getting to know their voices.

There is a difference between knowing the voice of a celebrity and knowing God's voice. You can know a celebrity's voice without knowing the celebrity. But you can't know God's voice without knowing God.

GOD WANTS YOU TO WANT TO KNOW HIM

Real Success Prayer #3: *Give me a passion to know You.*

The first step in knowing God is to meet Him. There must be a time in your life when you put your trust in Jesus Christ as your Lord and Savior. There is no relationship with Him apart from this important first step.

The Bible explains it this way:

God loves us—so much, in fact, that He allowed His Son to die for us.

> For God so loved the world that he gave his only Son, so that everyone who believes in him will not perish but have eternal life. (JOHN 3:16 NLT)

However, the Bible also tells us that we are all sinners and that sin keeps us from a personal relationship with God.

For all have sinned; all fall short of God's glorious standard. (RO-MANS 3:23 NLT)

In fact, there is nothing we can do to make ourselves right with God. The only legitimate payment for sin is death.

For the wages of sin is death, but the free gift of God is eternal life in Christ Jesus our Lord. (ROMANS 6:23)

And the only way for us to have a personal relationship with God is for Jesus to die and pay the price for our sins.

But God demonstrates His own love toward us, in that while we were yet sinners, Christ died for us. (ROMANS 5:8)

Because of His important sacrifice, the remaining step for us is to accept God's free gift of eternal life, believing He will do what He has promised.

If you confess with your mouth Jesus as Lord, and believe in your heart that God raised Him from the dead, you will be saved. (ROMANS 10:9)

But to all who believed him and accepted him, he gave the right to become children of God. (JOHN 1:12 NLT)

When you trust in Him, surrendering your life to Him, He will change you and make you a new person.

What this means is that those who become Christians become new persons. They are not the same anymore, for the old life is gone. A new life has begun! (2 CORINTHIANS 5:17 NLT)

GOD WANTS YOUR RELATIONSHIP WITH HIM TO PROGRESS

After you have met Christ personally, then you must invest time in getting to know Him. The only way for that to happen is for you to spend time in His Word, the Bible. It is God's way of speaking directly to you.

> All Scripture is inspired by God and is useful to teach us what is true and to make us realize what is wrong in our lives. It straightens us out and teaches us to do what is right. It is God's way of preparing us in every way, fully equipped for every good thing God wants us to do. (2 TIMOTHY 3:16–17 NLT)

It is crucial for you to invest time in God's Word, listening to His voice. Begin by setting aside a few minutes each day to read from a translation of the Bible that is easy for you to understand. Ask yourself questions as you read: What is this saying to me personally? Is this passage showing me something about my life? Let God speak personally to your heart through His Word.

Tennis star Michael Chang explains this process in his life. He says:

> *I do a Bible study first thing in the morning and also at night. Throughout the day, I'll pray—whenever—because the Lord is always there. Trying to stay close to the Lord can be very difficult to do by yourself, so you ask the Lord to help you. You ask Him to be your first love and your first priority.*[3]

Becoming familiar with His principles and precepts will cause you to hear His voice above all others. You will begin to learn and understand things from God's perspective. The psalmist said, "Open my eyes, that I may [see] wonderful things from Your law" (Psalm 119:18). You will also begin to notice that you have a growing desire to spend even more time with Him.

> I will give them a heart to know Me, for I am the Lord; and they will be My people, and I will be their God, for they will return to Me with their whole heart. (JEREMIAH 24:7)

It is as you grow to know Christ that you will become more like Him. Why is it some people who have been married a long time even begin to look like each other? Have you ever seen two

27

good friends who act the same? Maybe they laugh alike. The more time they spend with one another, the more they know each other's thoughts and feelings; and when they express themselves, their mannerisms and actions become very similar. That just demonstrates a basic Bible principle that says you become like the people you spend time with. And the more time you spend with the Lord, the more you will become like Him.

SUPPORT AND ENCOURAGEMENT IN THE LOCAL CHURCH

Real Success Prayer #4: *Lord, place me with other Christians where we can encourage and support one another.*

As you grow to become like Christ, it is also important to be involved in a local church. The church is where you find nurture, fellowship, encouragement, and support. It's a place where you grow through relationships with other Christians. There is much said throughout the New Testament about these relationships in the church. These principles are sometimes referred to as the *one another* of Scripture:

Love one another. (JOHN 15:12)
Be devoted to one another. (ROMANS 12:10)
Accept one another. (ROMANS 15:7)
Be patient . . . with one another. (EPHESIANS 4:2 NIV)
Be kind to one another. (EPHESIANS 4:32)
Forgive one . . . another. (COLOSSIANS 3:13 NIV)
Comfort one another. (1 THESSALONIANS 4:18)
Encourage one another. (1 THESSALONIANS 5:11)
Motivate one another. (See HEBREWS 10:24)
[Serve] one another. (1 PETER 4:10)

Get plugged into a church. Don't let the excuse of notoriety or the inconvenience of time keep you from experiencing this important part of your growth and development as a Christian. Find a church that teaches God's Word and feels strongly about evangelism and discipleship. Make church involvement a priority!

Another important factor in your process of growth is for you to be accountable to other Christians. The Bible says,

Iron sharpens iron, so one man sharpens another. (PROVERBS 27:17)

You need a close Christian friend who can help you see yourself honestly, pray for you, and encourage you.

Several years ago, I was invited along with a friend to speak to a citywide rally for the Fellowship of Christian Athletes. The rally was in a small town in Kansas, and we decided to drive there together. When we arrived, we were treated to dinner by the local sponsor of the rally, who happened to be one of those running fanatics. Before he took us to the homes where we would be staying, he asked if we wanted to get up at 6:00 the next morning and run five miles with him. We both told him he was crazy and needed help.

Early the next morning, I was awakened by a bright light and a loud voice. It was the local sponsor in my room, dressed in his running clothes, urging me to get up and run with him. I sleepily expressed my concern for his sanity and told him I would see him later in the day. That's when he told me my friend was waiting in the car and had said I was a wimp if I didn't go, too. Well, I didn't want to spend the trip home listening to him tell me that he ran and I didn't, so I grudgingly got up and went.

When I got to the car, my friend sat there glaring at me and said nothing. In fact, it was about the three-mile mark in our run before either one of us said anything. Finally, I looked at my friend and said to him, "I'll never forgive you. The only reason I'm doing this is because you are." He stopped and said to me, "What do you mean? I only got up this morning because you were already going." All of a sudden we both realized we'd been tricked. We had both been told the same story, which had caused us to get up early and run nearly five miles. I got up thinking he would be there, and he got up thinking I would be there.

I can't speak for my friend, but I can tell you what motivated me to get up that morning—it was accountability. I knew he would hold me accountable for what I did or didn't do. We all have a need for another Christian brother or sister to do the same for us in our spiritual lives.

You need someone to hold you accountable for your spiritual growth. You need a friend who will help you when you struggle and will motivate you to be all God wants you to be.

> Two people can accomplish more than twice as much as one; they get a better return for their labor. If one person falls, the other can reach out and help. But people who are alone when they fall are in real trouble. (ECCLESIASTES 4:9–10 NLT)

Spending time learning God's Word, getting involved in a local church, and staying accountable to a close Christian friend are all important parts of the process of becoming like Christ. This is the road to real success.

For the athlete, success is not about wins and losses or fame and financial gain. It's far greater. It's becoming all you can be. It's being the best possible athlete you can be, and that begins with becoming all God wants you to be. Now, that may involve winning. It may involve losing. It may mean becoming all-American, or it may mean being cut from your team. It may involve making a million dollars and getting your name in the headlines, or it may involve a career-ending injury or riding the bench.

The ultimate measure of real success is becoming like Jesus Christ.

To Think About

1. List some of the things that the world considers important in measuring success.

2. In what ways do the world's measurements fall short of real success?

3. What is the biblical definition of true success (Joshua 1:8–9)?

4. What does Romans 8:29 say about what God wants you to be?

5. What are some steps you can take to allow you to get to know God better?

DEFINING YOUR PURPOSE

**I RUN STRAIGHT TO
THE GOAL WITH PUR-
POSE IN EVERY STEP.**
(1 CORINTHIANS 9:26 NLT)

I bought a new pair of work gloves the other day. They're comfortable, and they're made of real leather. But I just can't seem to get them to do any work. The truth of the matter is, they won't pick up a rake, cut firewood, or do anything else until I put my hands inside them.

Now, I know that illustration seems pretty foolish, but it represents a very important point: *Purpose* is to an athlete as my hand is to the work glove. It is the determination, the inspiration, and the motivation for all the athlete is and all he does. Your purpose as an athlete is the central driving force behind your performance.

Concentrating on that motivating purpose allows you to perform with a singular focus, free from hindrances. Sport psychologist Shane Murphy emphasizes the importance of that kind of attitude when he says:

Concentration is the ability to focus all your attention on what you are doing. When you are fully concentrating, you are wholly absorbed in the present. You are not even aware that you are performing. You pay atten-

tion to only those things that are important, and distractions don't affect you.[1]

REAL SUCCESS INVOLVES PLEASING CHRIST

Real Success Prayer #5: *Give me a consuming desire to please You.*

If you're going to experience true success as an athlete, what should be your motivating purpose? What is it you should have as your single focus? The Bible gives some specific direction for the Christian looking for his or her purpose. Second Timothy 2:3–5 says, "Suffer hardship with me, as a good soldier of Christ Jesus. No soldier in active service entangles himself in the affairs of everyday life."

Why? "So that he may please the one who enlisted him as a soldier. And also if anyone competes as an athlete, he does not win the prize unless he competes according to the rules." Your purpose, if you're going to experience real success, must be to please the Lord. That is what must become your singular driving and motivating force.

How can this be accomplished? The best way is to picture only one fan in the stands. That lone fan is Jesus Christ. He is cheering you on and rooting for you. There are no other fans in the stands but He. No parents, no family, no friends, no scouts, and no media—just Jesus. Every aspect of your performance is directed to pleasing Him. Your attitudes are focused on pleasing Him. Your efforts are focused on pleasing Him—no one else.[2]

When my son was young, he played basketball in a league for small boys. There wasn't much to watch from a basketball perspective, but there was still plenty of entertainment. The games usually consisted of a lot of running up and down the court and very little scoring. Most of the boys were easily distracted, and my son was no exception. Every time he got his hands on the ball, he would look up to his mom and dad and grin from ear to ear. He was playing to please his parents.

Your key for success is to focus on pleasing only the Lord. And so, what is it that pleases Him? What pleases God about your performance as an athlete?

You may feel that winning the city championship is your priority and that you will please the Lord if you accomplish that specific goal. But in reality, although that may be a very good goal, it is really outside the realm of your control. And what takes place if that goal becomes your purpose in playing? What happens if, halfway through the season, your team is mathematically eliminated from the championship? How does that impact your performance as an athlete the rest of the season? If that goal has been your driving purpose, you have a problem.

Your goal may be simply to win the game. How does that impact your performance if, with five minutes to go, you are down by thirty points? If that goal has become your motivating purpose, it impacts you as an athlete.

Too many factors in winning are outside the realm of your control. You can't control how the referee calls the game or the poor performance of a teammate. You can't control how well your team will be coached or the obnoxious mouth of an opposing player. In fact, those things will become distractions that will keep you from maximum performance if you focus on them. That's why your purpose must be only to please Him. By focusing completely on pleasing the Lord, you are free from distractions that might hinder your performance.

Paul spoke correctly when he said in 2 Corinthians 5:9, "Therefore also we have as our ambition, whether at home or absent, to be pleasing to Him." "That's my purpose," said Paul, "to please God." What then is it that pleases God? What can you do to please Him that is within the realm of your control? The Bible gives several examples of what pleases the Lord.

GOD IS PLEASED WHEN
YOU SURRENDER YOUR HEART TO HIM

Real Success Prayer #6: *Make me into whatever You want me to be.*

Psalm 51:17 says, "The sacrifice you want is a broken spirit. A broken and repentant heart, O God, you will not despise" (NLT). If you want to please God as an athlete, surrender your life to Him.

One of my favorite things to play with when I was a kid was

Play-Doh. A few years back, when my kids were young, I got to re-live my childhood by playing with it all over again. Except for a few new colors, it really hasn't changed much. It still looks the same, feels the same, even tastes the same. (Oh, come on—you know what it tastes like, too!)

There is nothing like opening a brand-new can of Play-Doh. It's soft and pliable, and you can make anything out of it—anything you want. But if you don't keep the lid on the can, the Play-Doh will begin to harden and get crusty. When that happens, it is difficult to make anything out of it.

God is pleased when we surrender our hearts to Him by becoming soft and pliable in His hands, just like a brand-new can of Play-Doh. He can accomplish His plan in our lives when we say, "Here I am, God. Make anything out of me You want. Mold me into the person You want me to be."

Remember the old movies? When the bad guys had taken all the abuse they could from the good guys, they would stand up and wave a white flag. That was the way they let their opponents know they were surrendering.

The Bible tells us that if we want to please the Lord, we must surrender. It's really the opposite of the world's philosophy. Society will tell you, "Try harder." God says, "Give in." The world says, "Fight back." The Lord says, "Turn the other cheek." The world says, "Do it yourself." God says, "Let Me do it through you."

Unreasonable as it may seem, it's only when we surrender that the Lord is free to work through us with all of His mighty power. All of His resources and all of His strength are unleashed in our lives then. We're strongest when we surrender.

It is important you understand that God's first concern for you as an athlete is not winning, it is not gaining recognition, it is not making you happy or fulfilling all your dreams. His concern for your life is making you like Jesus. Let Him do His work. Surrender!

GOD IS PLEASED WHEN
YOU COMMIT YOURSELF TO SERVE HIM

Real Success Prayer #7: *Help me to experience true greatness in serving You.*

Paul writes in Galatians 1:10, "Obviously, I'm not trying to be a people pleaser! No, I am trying to please God. If I were still trying to please people, I would not be Christ's servant" (NLT).

Fifteen seconds to go in the game. It's the championship finals of the NCAA play-offs, and your team is down by one. The ball comes to you. You dribble past two men, spin around, and go up for the shot—soaring in slow motion. Three seconds . . . two . . . one . . . and *swish!* The shot goes in at the buzzer. Your team wins the championship, and it's all because of you!

A chance for greatness! We all have an idea of what it would be like to be great, but Jesus said that if you want to be great, you have to be a servant (Matthew 20:26). The key to greatness is serving others.

When it's all said and done, and the awards and medals have tarnished, there are very few who really achieve greatness. Jesus offers you an opportunity to be great. Will you accept it? Serve Him wholeheartedly!

Since being a servant pleases God, what are the characteristics of a servant athlete?

First of all, *a servant athlete understands that life is bigger than the game.* Darrell Porter, the MVP for the St. Louis Cardinals in the 1982 World Series, was interviewed after being awarded the honor. He said:

> *Happiness is not going to come from playing ball. Sooner or later, the game will humble you, no matter how big a shot you are. You better get your forever kind of happiness somewhere else.*[3]

The apostle Paul said it this way: "It is the Lord Christ whom you serve" (Colossians 3:24). The servant athlete sees a bigger picture. He looks beyond the game and keeps his focus on serving the Lord.

Second, *a servant athlete understands the team concept.* He knows his team needs him and he needs his team. The Bible describes the church, the body of Christ, in the same way:

> The human body has many parts, but the many parts make up only one body. So it is with the body of Christ. The eye can never say to

the hand, "I don't need you." The head can't say to the feet, "I don't need you." (1 CORINTHIANS 12:12, 21 NLT)

A. C. Green credits his high school coach with teaching him the concept of team play. He writes in his book *Victory:*

> *Coach Gray wouldn't allow me to be a hotshot scorer because he was more interested in the final stat—number one. He knew the only way we could reach that championship level was for us to become team players. In basketball and in life, everyone starts out with a what's-in-it-for-me attitude. Children are selfish. That natural selfishness has to be broken to be a winner. You have to realize you can't do it all by yourself. You need the team. Coach Gray made me pass the ball and play unselfishly. Regardless of the stats, we the team reached the top. We went all the way.*[4]

Third, *a servant athlete is an encourager to his or her teammates.* The Bible says, "Therefore encourage one another and build up one another" (1 Thessalonians 5:11). You should help your teammates to be their best.

While coaching a high school track team, I had a guy on the team who had very little athletic ability. He wound up running the long-distance runs and had finished dead last at every single meet we'd entered.

Finally, in an all-out effort to keep him from being last, I stationed members of the team all around the inside of the track for his race, so that he would never be out of earshot for an encouraging word. As he made his way around the track, the other team members cheered him on. Now, I'd like to tell you that my brilliant coaching strategy brought him an upset victory that day. The truth is, though, he didn't finish last. He beat two other guys. He was able to do it because of the encouragement of his fellow team members. In fact, without the team, it would have been the same old last place for him.

Finally, *a servant athlete is concerned about his teammates and those around him.* My neighbors across the street had their house burglarized. It took place in broad daylight while I sat in the living room of my house and while other people from the neighborhood drove by. The thieves pulled up to the garage with a truck, ransacked the house, and took off with all my neighbor's valuables. No one saw a thing. I didn't notice, and neither did any of the other neighbors.

Do you know why? It was really because, in this day and age, we aren't very involved in each other's lives. We live next door to folks and don't even know their names. The Bible tells us to make being together and knowing one another a priority. The reason is that we can't live alone, as if we're on an island. A servant knows he really needs other people. The servant athlete knows he really needs his teammates. The more involved we are in each other's lives, the more we can help one another. It is important to look out for your teammates.

GOD IS PLEASED WHEN
YOUR LIFESTYLE DEMONSTRATES HIM

Real Success Prayer #8: *Help me to be an example of You in my attitudes and actions.*

The Bible says in Colossians 1:10, "So that you will walk in a manner worthy of the Lord, to please Him in all respects, bearing fruit in every good work and increasing in the knowledge of God." That means your attitudes and actions on the field, your attitudes and actions in that meeting, and your attitudes and actions in that heated moment of competition. A lifestyle that demonstrates Him— that's what pleases Him, the only fan in the stands.

In Charles Sheldon's classic book *In His Steps,* an entire community experiences dramatic change when a group of Christians make some lifestyle-changing determinations. They resolve that before they make any decisions in their lives, they will ask the question, What would Jesus do? Then they will do it His way.

It might be good as an athlete to ask the question, What would Jesus do? How would Jesus respond to a cheap elbow in a basketball game? How would Jesus handle a horrible call by the referee? What would be His response to defeat? We know Jesus said, "But I tell you, Do not resist an evil person. If someone strikes you on the right cheek, turn to him the other also" (Matthew 5:39 NIV). What will you do in that situation so that your lifestyle demonstrates Him?

How would Jesus deal with the issue of competing for the same position with another teammate? Remember, the Bible says we are to encourage one another and build up one another. What difference will that make in your life if your desire is to please the Lord?

The bottom line is: If you are going to please the Lord, then your words and your actions will be an example of Jesus Christ. You must allow Him to change any area of your life that is not consistent with the truths of His Word. This pleases the Lord and brings true success for you as a Christian athlete.

> And whatever you do or say, let it be as a representative of the Lord Jesus, all the while giving thanks through him to God the Father. (COLOSSIANS 3:17 NLT)

GOD IS PLEASED WHEN
YOU RELY ON HIM COMPLETELY

Real Success Prayer #9: *Help me to depend on You to be my source of strength.*

The Bible tells us that without faith it is impossible to please God (Hebrews 11:6). That means in the midst of a setback, in the midst of an injury, in the midst of a defeat, in the midst of a failure, you can put your trust wholeheartedly in Him. That is what pleases Him.

In 1964, Houston's Ken Johnson pitched a no-hitter against the Cincinnati Reds. A no-hitter is the single greatest accomplishment for a pitcher in the game of baseball. The only problem with Ken Johnson's no-hitter is that the Reds beat Houston that night 1–0, because Ken's team made two errors in the game that allowed Cincinnati to score the winning run. His performance was the best he could possibly manage, but it wasn't good enough.

That goes to show that you can try your very best, but sometimes it just isn't enough. The real issue here is relying on God, whatever happens. The Bible calls it trust. It's allowing God to work through you to accomplish His purpose—to do something in and through you that you could never have accomplished yourself—even at your best. That pleases Him.

One afternoon I had to dig up a tree in my front yard. It was just a small evergreen tree, but it was one of the toughest jobs I've ever tackled. I dug around awhile, then chopped off a few roots; dug around a little more and chopped off a few more roots. But the tree still wouldn't budge. I probably cut off fifty roots with no real progress. Eventually, I succeeded in digging underneath the tree, and I found the main root. After a lot of sweat, blisters, and sore muscles, I finally dug up that little tree. The deep roots had made the difference.

The Bible says the person who relies on God and His Word will be like a tree that's firmly planted, whose roots go down deep. Strong winds won't budge him. Difficulty won't shake him. Career setbacks won't uproot him. He has an unshakable foundation.

Your life can be like that tree. Ask God to put some roots down deep in your life. Depend on Him for everything and in every situation. Stay in His Word. Allow Him to be the source of your strength in everything you do. Then your life will withstand any storm.

> Oh, the joys of those who do not follow the advice of the wicked, or stand around with sinners, or join in with scoffers. But they delight in doing everything the Lord wants; day and night they think about his law. They are like trees planted along the riverbank, bearing fruit each season without fail. Their leaves never wither, and in all they do, they prosper. (PSALM 1:1–3 NLT)

If it is your desire to experience real success, learn what pleases God and focus your performance on the one fan in the stands— Jesus Christ. Let every aspect of your attitudes and actions bring glory and honor to Him. Then you will be on the road to true success.

> For God is working in you, giving you the desire to obey him and the power to do what pleases him. (PHILIPPIANS 2:13 NLT)

41

To Think About

1. Rate the following as motivating factors for you in your athletic performance:

   Pleasing friends or family (parents, girlfriend, boyfriend, spouse, coach, etc.)
   1 — 2 — 3 — 4 — 5 — 6 — 7 — 8 — 9 — 10

   Recognition (name in the paper, awards, scholarships, etc.)
   1 — 2 — 3 — 4 — 5 — 6 — 7 — 8 — 9 — 10

   Being the best
   1 — 2 — 3 — 4 — 5 — 6 — 7 — 8 — 9 — 10

   Financial gain
   1 — 2 — 3 — 4 — 5 — 6 — 7 — 8 — 9 — 10

   Winning
   1 — 2 — 3 — 4 — 5 — 6 — 7 — 8 — 9 — 10

2. How can these motivating factors hinder your athletic performance?

3. What are some characteristics of a servant athlete? Which of these do you need to improve in your life?

4. What about your attitudes and actions as an athlete that are pleasing to God?

5. Do any of your attitudes and actions as an athlete not please God?

REMOVING THE OBSTACLES

$\int$uppose you are watching the track-and-field events at the Olympics. The greatly anticipated 100-meter finals is the next event on the schedule. The runners have been stretching and are ready to take the blocks. Each one is prepared to run his best.

However, your eyes are drawn to one lone runner, and you notice that something is not quite right. Next to the other sprinters, he stands out like a sore thumb. As they are set to race in their sleek running outfits and specially crafted shoes, he is wearing jeans, a sweater, and cowboy boots. Seem ridiculous? What athlete would expect to seriously compete while wearing an outfit that would hinder his performance?

The second part of your strategy for real success is to remove the obstacles that keep you from being all you need to be so that you can please the Lord. The writer of Hebrews says:

> Therefore, since we are surrounded by such a huge crowd of witnesses to the life of faith, let us strip off every weight that slows us down, especially the sin that so easily hinders our progress. And let us run

with endurance the race that God has set before us. We do this by keeping our eyes on Jesus, on whom our faith depends from start to finish. (HEBREWS 12:1–2 NLT)

The Bible says to strip off weights and sins. These are the things that hold you back and hinder your performance. What is it that hinders you as an athlete from being everything God wants you to be? What are those sins, those weights for you? How can you identify them?

GOD WILL HELP YOU
SEE WHERE YOU NEED TO CHANGE

Real Success Prayer #10: *Lord, examine my desires, attitudes, and actions. Show me anything that is keeping me from being what You want me to be. Lead me down Your path.*

Psalm 139:23–24 provides the perfect prayer for the athlete who desires to remove distractions and encumbrances. The verses say, "Search me, O God, and know my heart; try me and know my anxious thoughts; and see if there be any hurtful way in me, and lead me in the everlasting way." It is a three-part prayer.

The first part of the prayer is asking the Lord to take a good long look at you. There is no one who knows you better. He sees every detail of your life.

O Lord, you have searched me and you know me. You know when I sit and when I rise; you perceive my thoughts from afar. You discern my going out and my lying down; you are familiar with all my ways. Before a word is on my tongue you know it completely, O Lord. (PSALM 139:1–4 NIV)

The second part of the prayer asks God to point out anything that is an obstacle to His plan for you. He will help you see things you never realized were there. Dallas Cowboys safety Bill Bates shares an experience from early in his Christian life:

Because I seriously started trusting the Lord, I began to see little changes in my life. One of the most significant changes I recall is reaching a deci-

sion about how I would treat other people. I had never been purposely cruel to people, but I still had some of that "bully" from my playground days inside of me. From reading my Bible, I learned that Jesus was not a bully—so I didn't need to be one either! I started treating people with more respect and, in doing so, found that people treated me better as well. It was very encouraging to see my Christianity at work in my everyday life.[1]

God will point out specific things in your life that are not pleasing to Him. It is His desire to change those areas of your life from the inside out. The Bible says:

> Don't copy the behavior and customs of this world, but let God transform you into a new person by changing the way you think. Then you will know what God wants you to do, and you will know how good and pleasing and perfect his will really is. (ROMANS 12:2 NLT)

Third, it is asking God to lead you down His path and allowing Him to guide your way. It is praying that you will not be distracted but stay focused on His plan. Psalm 27:11 says, "Teach me Your way, O Lord, and lead me in a level path."

I was at a conference in Nashville and stayed at the famous Opryland Hotel. What a place! It's like being in a multibuilding hotel inside the Superdome. It's huge!

I checked in, and the guy at the desk showed me on a map how to find my room. He pointed out all of the turns I was to take and the landmarks to help me find my way. So I headed off, carrying my two bags, in search of my room. After about fifteen minutes, I noticed I had passed the same landmark several times. I stopped, checked the map the man at the front desk had given me, checked my landmarks, and tried to get back to where I started. It didn't work—I was lost.

After a few more minutes of wandering, I found someone with an employee's name tag and pleaded for help. I must have looked pretty worn out, because he was kind enough to take one of my bags and walk me to my room. The point is, the map had shown me the way, but it wasn't enough. I also needed someone to lead me. That's exactly what God wants to do for you. He will help you to see the path you need to take, and He will also take you by the hand and lead you down that path.

Make this three-part prayer a regular part of your routine. Allow God to show you the areas that need to be changed, and let Him help you change. It is a surefire plan for true success against the obstacles in your life.

Obviously, any sin is a hindrance to a Christian, and things such as sexual immorality, drugs, and alcohol can have a harmful impact on an athlete. However, these and other destructive influences can be summarized into three categories. I call them the "three deadly sins" for any athlete. These three will immediately hinder a maximum performance. They are quite common and can be seen in almost any competition. The three are anger, pride, and lack of self-control.

ANGER

My son, Nathan, played in a summer basketball league against a young man who had a tremendous amount of talent. Nathan was always able to get the best of him, though, because every time the referee made a call the guy didn't agree with, he would get mad. Whenever someone scored on him or his shot wasn't falling, his temper would take over. That would generally result in a technical, or he would become so frustrated that he would begin to play out of control.

How many times have you seen it? In the midst of a game, the referee makes a call an athlete doesn't agree with, and he loses his cool. And what happens when he loses his cool? At that moment he ceases to be a focused athlete. He's distracted, and he can't reach his full potential because he's too angry to focus his attention on his job. A basketball player misses a layup, and while he is slamming the wall with his fist, the guy on the other team is halfway down the court for two points. Anger takes away your focus from being the best you can be and hinders your performance. The Bible says anger puts you in a dangerous position. "Like a city that is broken into and without walls is a man who has no control over his spirit" (Proverbs 25:28).

What can you do to control your anger? I want to suggest four success steps to victory that will help if you struggle in this area.

Stay away from angry people. Proverbs 22:24–25 says, "Do not associate with a man given to anger; or go with a hot-tempered man, or you will learn his ways, and find a snare for yourself." In other words, if you hang out with hotheads, you'll be like them.

Now, I realize that it's not always possible to stay away from folks who lose their cool. We don't always choose our teammates or coaches. But you need to realize that you are influenced by your environment. If you are in an angry environment, you will have to work harder in this area.

Guard your mouth. Proverbs 21:23 tells us, "He who guards his mouth and his tongue, guards his soul from troubles." Proverbs 13:3 says, "The one who guards his mouth preserves his life; the one who opens wide his lips comes to ruin." It is important to keep a close watch on your mouth.

In 1976, a man from Tulsa, Oklahoma, stood trial for attempted robbery. He had been accused of snatching a woman's purse, and, feeling confident of his persuasive speaking ability, he decided to act as his own lawyer. While questioning the victim during the trial, he asked, "Did you get a good look at my face when I took your purse?" He was later convicted and sent to prison.

Have you ever said something you wished you could take back? That fellow is an obvious example, but most of us have been guilty of talking without thinking at least a few times.

The Bible says to guard your lips. Watch carefully what you say! Your words have the potential to destroy reputations, friendships, or entire families. They can put you at odds with your teammates, get you into trouble, and ruin your witness for Christ. They can even destroy you. Those words are ones usually spoken without thinking. Wouldn't it be a good idea to learn to stand guard over what we say?

Choose not to get angry. This may seem pretty simple, but it is your decision to get angry and your decision not to get angry. In Proverbs 19:11 we learn that "a man's discretion makes him slow to anger, and it is his glory to overlook a transgression."

A newspaper recently reported the unique story of a guy who had a difficult time passing the test for his driver's license. In fact, he had failed the test six times in a row. The seventh try found him in jail, charged with assault. You see, when he turned in the test to the examiner, he misunderstood him to say that he had flunked again, when, in fact, the man was trying to tell him that he had finally passed. He became so angry that he injured the examiner by hitting him over the head with the first thing he could pick up.

The man missed a huge victory because he could not control his temper long enough to discover the truth. If he had just listened before he acted! He was a fool. Scripture tells us not to be so easily provoked. If we can't control our anger, the Bible says, we are fools (Proverbs 29:11).

How about you? Do you act before you think? Is it too easy for you to get angry? The choice is yours. It is your decision to control your anger. Don't be a fool!

Memorize Scripture. Psalm 119:11 reads, "Your word I have treasured in my heart, that I may not sin against You." One of the best ways to gain victory in an area of struggle is to memorize Scripture. There are many verses to commit to memory on the subject of overcoming anger. The following are good ones to learn. Most are from the *New Living Translation.*

PSALM 37:8: Stop your anger! Turn from your rage! Do not envy others —it only leads to harm.

PROVERBS 14:17: Those who are short-tempered do foolish things, and schemers are hated.

PROVERBS 15:1: A gentle answer turns away wrath, but harsh words stir up anger.

PROVERBS 15:18: A hothead starts fights; a cool-tempered person tries to stop them.

PROVERBS 16:32: He who is slow to anger is better than the mighty, and he who rules his spirit, than he who captures a city (NASB).

PROVERBS 19:11: People with good sense restrain their anger; they earn esteem by overlooking wrongs.

COLOSSIANS 3:8: But now is the time to get rid of anger, rage, malicious behavior, slander, and dirty language.

EPHESIANS 4:26: And don't sin by letting anger gain control over you.

PRIDE

When I was growing up, I played with a guy who would get distracted if he thought he wasn't going to be the leading scorer in the game. If someone else on the team was having a good game, he would start tossing up bad shots—anything to be the top guy. Ultimately that behavior would hurt the team and, unbeknownst to him, his quest to be number one.

Pride is playing as if *you* are the only fan in the stands. Pride is an encumbrance that will keep you from being all you can be. It will make you too concerned about what others think and will distract you from your focus as an athlete. When you're playing to please only yourself, the Bible says, you have set some careless guidelines for your life. The Scripture says, "Pride goes before destruction, and a haughty spirit before stumbling" (Proverbs 16:18).

The opposite of pride is humility. It is a characteristic God wants to develop in your life. The best living definition I have ever known for the word "humility" is my friend Ed Stephenson. Ed, while a senior at Tulsa University, hit more home runs than any other college baseball player in the entire nation. In fact, he still holds the record for home runs at TU, and his name can still be found in the NCAA record books.

What's so unusual is that I knew Ed for several years and never knew about his accomplishments. He never did tell me. Someone else told me. He had reason to brag about himself, but he didn't. The Bible tells us not to toot our own horn. Jesus said everyone who does will be humbled, but he who humbles himself will be exalted (Matthew 23:12). Pride takes away your focus; humility allows you to stay properly focused on pleasing God.

Some have the idea that humility means timidity—a kind of Casper Milquetoast attitude that puts forth a halfhearted effort. That couldn't be further from the truth. All-star major leaguer Kevin Seitzer explains:

When I started reading the Scripture about being humble, I started real-izing I had to get after it and to be all I can be as a Christian; be a witness as a baseball player and a husband and a father; and use everything He has given me and made me in order to bring honor to Him.²

How do we combat the obstacle of pride in our lives? Here are three true success steps to victory that will produce humility in your life:

The first step to humility is to realize who you are in comparison to God. You are not God—not even close. When you see yourself in light of the awesomeness of the one true, living God, it helps to keep your imagined awesomeness in perspective.

He who forms the mountains, creates the wind, and reveals his thoughts to man, he who turns dawn to darkness, and treads the high places of the earth—the Lord God Almighty is his name. (AMOS 4:13 NIV)

Did you build anything with Tinkertoys when you were a kid? Did it look like the picture on the box when you were finished? If you were like most kids, it didn't. In fact, if you tried it today, it prob-ably still wouldn't look much like the picture. Well, what if you tried building a space shuttle in your backyard or a computer in your garage? Could you do it? How about a tree, or a mountain, or maybe a star? What about a person? No way. Impossible.

But God can make a tree, sculpture a mountain, and make the likes of you from scratch—and He did! You may think it's really something that you can shoot a basketball or hit a baseball or run fast, but remember it is God who created you and shaped you phys-ically. Your part is small! His part is impressive!

For You formed my inward parts; You wove me in my mother's womb. I will give thanks to You, for I am fearfully and wonderfully made; wonderful are Your works, and my soul knows it very well. My frame was not hidden from You, when I was made in secret, and skillfully wrought in the depths of the earth; Your eyes have seen my unformed substance; and in Your book were all written the days that were or-dained for me, when as yet there was not one of them. (PSALM 139:13–16)

When I served on the staff of a large church, occasionally, some unusual people would wander through the doors during office hours. Some were looking for money, and others were just looking for someone to listen to their story.

Late one afternoon, the receptionist called me, needing help with a rather loud person in her office. I went out and beheld one of the most intimidating men I had ever seen. He stood about 6 foot 10 inches with shoulder-length hair, a long beard, and was dressed in a black suit. He said he was a prophet and wanted to talk to me.

We sat down in my office, and he proceeded to talk uninterrupted for almost an hour. The more he talked, the louder he got, and I was getting a little concerned about getting out in one piece. He told me he had caused earthquakes, floods, droughts—in fact, he claimed credit for just about every major disaster in the last fifteen years. The bottom line was that he wanted me to give him money or he would snap his fingers and the wrath of God would come down upon me.

I finally looked him in the eye and said, "Friend, no man snaps his fingers and makes God do anything. He snaps His fingers, and you take a breath. He snaps them twice, and you never breathe again." When I finished saying that, his face changed, he thanked me, and left quietly.

Now, I'm not sure what his racket was—if he was crazy, demon possessed, or just a con artist, but for a moment he realized who he was in comparison to an awesome God. Remember to keep that in perspective in your life, too.

The second step to humility is to be teachable. While I was in college, soccer was added to the list of varsity sports at our school. I want to be careful not to date myself, but this was before soccer had gained the popularity in the States that it has today. The coach that the athletic director appointed for the team was an assistant in a couple of other sports but knew very little about soccer.

As I followed the team closely, it was interesting to observe a young player who had grown up in South America. He had played the sport all of his life. If there was anyone on the team who was in a position to treat the coach with disrespect or ridicule his approach, it would have been this fellow. He knew far more about the game than the inexperienced coach. However, he chose to learn whatever he could from this coach, and his teachable attitude made a difference in the entire team.

On the other hand, I once coached a young man in high school who had tremendous talent and natural ability. On a bad day he was better than most. Playing ball came easy to him. However, because of his outstanding ability, he didn't feel it necessary to work as hard as anyone else. He didn't take extra swings in the batting cage, because he didn't need to. He put in the minimum amount of practice. Ultimately, he never became all he could have become. He wasn't teachable.

The Bible says, "A wise man will hear and increase in learning, and a man of understanding will acquire wise counsel" (Proverbs 1:5). A teachable athlete, one who is willing to learn and continue learning, is an athlete who experiences real success.

The third step to humility involves remembering the source of your ability. A women's volleyball player from the University of Oklahoma told me that her greatest struggle, after working hard and seeing that effort pay off, was keeping in perspective that God had blessed her with the resources to achieve athletically great things for Him. Cy Young award winner Randy Johnson came to grips with this as well. He said:

> *There are a lot of professional athletes who think they're doing it all on their own. I was one of those athletes at one time. I felt that when I struck out a bunch of guys, that it was solely me doing it—but not anymore. The Lord's given me the ability to go out and do the things that I do.[3]*

It is easy to get caught up in your accomplishments and your abilities, but you must remember who has blessed you with the capacity to perform. After winning his first Grand Slam title, Michael Chang publicly gave thanks to Jesus Christ, saying, "Without Him, I'm nothing!"[4] Jesus said it this way, "I am the vine, you are the branches; he who abides in Me, and I in him, he bears much fruit, for apart from Me you can do nothing" (John 15:5). He blesses you with the ability, and you use that ability to bring glory and honor to Him.

A LACK OF SELF-CONTROL

It is commonplace to read in the newspaper about an athlete being ejected from a game for losing control. Professional athletes have amassed literally millions of dollars in fines and suspensions due to fights and other obnoxious behavior.

Recently a top college prospect from a high school in a large metropolitan area was arrested for punching a referee. The ref had called two technical fouls on him, causing him to be ejected from the basketball game, so the player hit him with a right hook. The young man was arrested and charged with assault. His college career was greatly jeopardized.

Several promising high school athletes from a nearby community thought it would really be fun to steal a case of beer from a convenience store late one night. Two guys waited with the car running, while two more ran into the store and captured the prize before the clerk could respond. They jumped into the car and sped off in a cloud of dust. After laughing it up and enjoying their seemingly harmless prank, they began to feel some remorse and decided to return the goods to the store. However, before they got back to the parking lot, they were stopped by the police and arrested for theft. Ultimately the young men were only required to do community service as a punishment for their crime, but their encounter with the law resulted in suspension from school. It also brought an end to their high school athletic careers and the possibility of a college scholarship for one of them.

The Bible says, "A person without self-control is as defenseless as a city with broken-down walls" (Proverbs 25:28 NLT). If you are going to experience true success, you must learn self-control. The apostle Paul uses an illustration from the life of an athlete when he says:

> Remember that in a race everyone runs, but only one person gets the prize. You also must run in such a way that you will win. All athletes practice self-control. They do it to win a prize that will fade away, but we do it for an eternal prize. So I run straight to the goal with purpose in every step. I am not like a boxer who misses his punches. I

discipline my body like an athlete, training it to do what it should. (1 CORINTHIANS 9:24–27 NLT)

Paul says the athlete's answer to the problem of self-control is discipline. For the athlete, the recipe for discipline is good old-fashioned hard work and the determination to do the right thing. A. C. Green writes:

You must have discipline to reach a championship level in life. In professional basketball, if a player has talent and ability but doesn't have discipline, he washes out. Anyone can do something once, but not well. Maybe after a lot of tries, someone can do something perfectly a time or two. But to do something perfectly every time requires constant practice, and practice requires discipline. Coach Pat Riley always worked our Laker teams to the point of fatigue at practice. His reasoning was that we had to be able to shoot and execute plays as well at the end of the game, when we were tired, as we did at the beginning, when we were fresh. Discipline made us a championship team. Discipline will take what you master or acquire and keep it for you.[5]

You must discipline yourself to control your attitudes and actions both on and off the field of competition. It begins on the inside. Paul writes:

Spend your time and energy in training yourself for spiritual fitness. Physical exercise has some value, but spiritual exercise is much more important, for it promises a reward in both this life and the next. (1 TIMOTHY 4:7–8 NLT)

In conclusion, you can't experience true success without removing the obstacles that keep you from becoming all God wants you to be. Just as a sprinter wearing street clothes is unable to do his best, you must work to eliminate the things that slow you down. Let Him show you the areas of your life that hinder your success and allow Him to change you.

To Think About

1. What are some examples of how you have seen anger hinder an athlete's performance?

2. Which of the four victory steps over anger do you need to work on the most?

3. What are some examples you have seen of pride hindering someone's athletic performance?

4. What areas in your life would benefit from a dose of humility?

5. What are some examples you have seen of a lack of self-control hindering someone's athletic performance?

6. As you work to remove these unnecessary weights from your life, what level of effort should you put forth? How much does it take to experience true success?

GIVING YOUR ALL

The first of my children to play basketball was my daughter, Ashley. She started playing in the fifth grade and played through her seventh-grade year. The games were rarely high scoring or fast paced, but they provided some of my favorite sports memories.

In spite of the fact that Ashley wasn't very big and didn't score often, watching her was always the highlight of the game. The best moments were when she would play what I called her bumblebee defense. She would get right up in the face of the player she was guarding and wave her arms wildly. Sometimes her arms moved so fast they were just a blur. There is no doubt in my mind that if a bumblebee played basketball, it would play like Ashley. She never quit, never let up, and her arms never slowed down. Her all-out style was always distracting to the opposing player and often resulted in a turnover.

We learn from Ashley's bumblebee defense an important aspect of our strategy for real success: giving your all. The successful athlete gives a maximum performance. It is a wholehearted, 110 percent, all-out, nothing-left-to-give effort. Colossians 3:23–24 says it very well. "Whatever you do, do your work heartily, as for the Lord rather than for men, knowing that from the Lord you will receive the reward of the inheritance. It is the Lord Christ whom you serve."

He is the One that you must please, and He is pleased and glorified through wholehearted effort.

Dallas Cowboys defensive tackle Chad Hennings understands this principle of true success. He says:

> *Part of my commitment to Jesus is that in everything I do, I give 100 percent. That's how I can glorify Him. Anything less than that is doing myself and my Lord a disservice. Christ gave His all for me in everything He did—from leaving the Father to dying on the cross to taking care of my needs now—so the very least I can do is give Him my all in everything I do. Not to repay Him; that would be as foolish as it was impossible. But I give Him my all because I love Him.[1]*

WHOLEHEARTED PREPARATION

Your diligence as a Christian athlete can be seen in two ways: in your preparation and in your performance. Wholehearted preparation is a foundational principle taught in the Bible. Scripture stresses the value of practice and preparedness.

> Prepare your work outside and make it ready for yourself in the field; afterwards, then, build your house. (PROVERBS 24:27)

When my son was in the seventh grade, he went out for basketball. He had worked very hard and really wanted to make the A team. The first day of practice, however, more than one hundred kids were out for basketball, and it seemed to him that the football stars were the only ones being looked at by the coaches.

Still, he believed that his hard work would pay off and that if the coaches could just *see* him, he had a good chance to make the team. So he decided that after practice he would challenge the coach to a game. Every day he played one-on-one with the coach. The coach saw his ability, and it won him a starting spot on the B team. After several games, he was moved up to the A team.

A diligent effort in practice and preparation will always pay off. Proverbs 22:29 says, "Do you see a man skilled in his work?

He will stand before kings; he will not stand before obscure men." All great athletes have known the value of wholehearted preparation. Roger Maris once said, "You hit home runs not by chance but by preparation." Legendary coach Pop Warner constantly reminded his players that they play the way they practice. You will never be successful in a game without wholehearted effort in practice.

All-pro defensive end Reggie White comments on the importance of hard work, saying,

> I believe in being the absolute best you can be at whatever you do. "Good enough" is never good enough. Constantly strive to improve. Don't just show up; be a champion. Whatever "game" you are playing—teaching, coaching, parenting, running a business, entertaining, preaching, whatever— make it a Super Bowl performance![2]

John Wooden coached the men's basketball team at UCLA to ten national championships. He had this to say about preparation: "Hard work is essential, and only you really know if you're giving it everything you've got. People who always try to cut corners will never come close to realizing their full potential."[3]

One of the most dramatic examples of commitment to wholehearted preparation is seen in the early life of Pete Maravich. Pete's experience is recounted in his book *Heir to a Dream*.

> When I was thirteen years old I spent most of the year in the old gymnasium of the YMCA. It was my world; my solitude and fortress; my home away from home. Day after day, for hours on end, I practiced shooting, ball handling, dribbling, and passing in the old gym. During the summer months I was almost always alone. Total dedication to basketball isolated me from most of my friends. But as far as I was concerned, I didn't really need the company unless they were interested in a game of one-on-one. That was rarely the case.
>
> I spent thousands of hours practicing basketball in the YMCA. To break the monotony I attempted anything I could think of to do with a basketball. I began shooting numerous trick shots such as bouncing the ball off the wall and the ceiling, getting it to ricochet into the basket. I was only limited by my imagination.

Whenever Dad saw boredom setting in, his creativity pushed me, elim-
inating it. He even had me stretch out the passenger side of our car and
try to control my dribble as he drove at various speeds.[4]

It is no wonder that Maravich went on to set numerous NCAA
scoring records, get elected to the Basketball Hall of Fame, and is
considered one of the greatest players of all time. Practice produces
results, and wholehearted practice produces true success.

WHOLEHEARTED PERFORMANCE

God is glorified through your athletic ability when you compete
wholeheartedly. It is like my daughter's bumblebee defense. He is
honored when, from start to finish, you never quit, never lose your
focus, and never give up. Your maximum effort brings Him maximum glory.

The story of Eric Liddell, the great Scottish Olympian who gave
his life on the mission field in China, was portrayed in the Academy-
Award-winning film *Chariots of Fire*. One of my favorite scenes from
that movie centers on a pre-Olympic 440-yard race where Liddell falls
on the track but gets up to finish, obviously giving his all. Catherine
Swift tells of that true incident in her biography, *Eric Liddell*:

The race started on the bend with Eric on the inside. The starting pistol
sounded and everyone got off to a good start—for the first three strides.

Then Gillies, one of the English runners, tripped and crashed into Eric
sending him stumbling from the track onto the grass verge at the side. The
crowd gasped in horror. Eric seemed stunned. Bitterly disappointed and
sure of disqualification—although it clearly had been an accident—he
came to a halt. Then he noticed the officials frantically signaling to him.
For a moment he tried to make out what they were saying.

Suddenly he understood. They were telling him to carry on. But Eric
knew it wasn't possible to catch up. His leading opponents were already
twenty yards ahead. Yet, as if spurred on by some superior force, the plucky
athlete leapt back on to the track. Again the crowd gasped as he thun-
dered along. Everyone knew no one could make up the difference.

Still, he went on and on. Spectators gaped wide-eyed, their hearts pump-
ing as fast as his own.

When the runners had reached the home stretch, Eric Liddell had not only caught up—he was placing fourth, a mere ten yards behind Gillies. At that point his strength visibly began to ebb away and it was obvious he was about to collapse. He set his teeth hard and from somewhere deep inside came some super-human energy. Instead of crumpling to the ground, he carried on. He fought for breath. His knees came up ever higher and his fists thumped out at the air as though trying to cut a way through it. In a flash he was running third, second, then finally he shot ahead of Gillies to win the race by two yards.

The onlookers were near hysterics. They rose to their feet as one person, clapping and cheering for Eric Liddell, a man who had achieved the impossible in the face of absolute defeat.[5]

The Christian athlete is able to give a wholehearted performance when he removes the distractions and hindrances so that he can remain focused on his single purpose: to please the only fan in the stands, Jesus Christ.

Therefore, since we have so great a cloud of witnesses surrounding us, let us also lay aside every encumbrance and the sin which so easily entangles us, and *let us run with endurance the race that is set before us, fixing our eyes on Jesus.* (HEBREWS 12:1, italics added)

Orel Hershiser gives his perspective on wholehearted performance when he says:

To call myself a Christian and then not strive to be the best I can be and do the most I can with what God has given me would be the height of hypocrisy. Being a Christian is no excuse for mediocrity or passive acceptance of defeat. If anything, Christianity demands a higher standard, more devotion to the task.

Before I was a Christian winning and losing were my only gauges for success. Now I know that diligence and execution are every bit as important. I can be satisfied and successful if I do what is right—preparing mentally and physically and using proper mechanics and strategy—even if I lose.[6]

You may not know the name William Booth, yet his work can be seen all around the world nearly one hundred years after he lived. General William Booth was the founder of the Salvation Army. The success of this outstanding ministry can be traced to one central issue—he gave his all for the Lord. Shortly before his death, he revealed the key to his success:

> *I will tell you the secret, God has had all there was of me. There have been men with greater brains than I, men with greater opportunities. But from the day I got the poor of London on my heart and caught a vision of all Jesus Christ could do with them, on that day I made up my mind that God would have all of William Booth there was. And if there is anything of power in the Salvation Army today, it is because God has all the adoration of my heart, all the power of my will, and all the influences of my life.[7]*

One of the greatest lessons I've ever learned in this area I learned through some unusual circumstances. One Sunday morning I was getting ready to go out and preach in a church in a little town out in Kansas. Before starting off, I was thumbing through my desk looking for something, and I found a surprise that I wasn't looking for. My phone bill. It was Sunday, and the charges were due on Monday. The total bill was for $26.18. Well, the problem was that I had just taken all the money I had, all my quarters, all my change, everything, and put it in the gas tank of my car so I could get out to this church. So I prayed, "Lord, I'm gonna have to depend on You to help me with that phone bill." I grabbed my Bible and headed for the car.

I got to the church, and the pastor met me at the door. He thanked me for coming and told me that during the service they were going to take a love offering for me to help with my expenses. I thanked him while trying to hide my excitement and silently reminded God about the phone bill.

After the service, I was standing at the back door shaking hands with people as they came out. The last person out the door was the chairman of the deacons. He shook my hand, slapped a wad of bills in my hand, and said, "Mike, this is the money that was in the offering plate this morning. We hope it helps you out with your expenses." It was a total of $26.16.

Giving Your All

Now, you will remember that the phone bill is $26.18. That's two cents short. Well, you know how every once in a while you'll find a penny lying on the ground? I walked around all day looking for pennies. I wound up borrowing a couple of cents from my roommate, and the next morning I paid the phone bill.

And so I got to thinking, what's the lesson from that story? What is God trying to tell me through that experience? Is it that God wants us to give our two cents' worth? No, that's too corny. Actually, that is the problem. Too many times all we give God is two cents' worth of our lives. Two cents' worth of prayer; two cents' worth of fellowship; two cents' worth of Bible study; two cents' worth of effort. And yet we're always expecting God to provide the full $26.18! Well, that's not the way God wants it. He wants our all, not two cents' worth.

A few weeks later, still a poor college student, I was sitting in the worship service at my own church on Sunday morning, and the time came for the offering. The offering plate came by, and I reached for my wallet. The only problem was that all I had was a ten-dollar bill. No fives, no ones, no quarters, nothing but a ten-dollar bill. That's it.

So I thought, *This is all I've got, and I'm not sure when I'm going to get anymore. You know, Lord, I'm gonna have to catch You later or something.* By the way, it never looks good taking change out of the collection plate. They always look at you real funny. So I thought, *OK. This afternoon I will get some change, and I'll come back tonight.* No problem. Right?

I went out to eat and came back to church that night. Truthfully, I had forgotten all about the money until the time came for the offering. The offering plate came by. I pulled out my wallet, opened it up, and all I had was a five-dollar bill. I couldn't believe this was happening to me. All I could think of was *This is all the money I have!* So I just put my wallet back in my pocket, and the plate went by, and I mumbled silently, *I'm sorry, God, but all I had to give was all I have* . . . and then it hit me. All I have to give is all I have. But all I have is what He wants.

Trust in the Lord with all your heart and do not lean on your own understanding. In all your ways acknowledge Him, and He will make your paths straight. (PROVERBS 3:5–6)

63

God wants your all—a total commitment of your life and your efforts for Him. It begins in your heart and continues through every aspect of your life. As an athlete, it is best seen through your maximum effort, not by the results of your performance. It's a bumblebee approach to all you do. That is a mark of real success.

To Think About

1. Are you more likely to give more effort during a game or during practice?

2. Which area is more important?

3. Read Colossians 3:23–24. What does this verse tell you about whatever you do?

4. What areas in your life need wholehearted effort?

6

FOCUSING ON JESUS

As a junior high boy I wanted to be Pistol Pete Maravich. I watched him play every time he was on television. I practiced dribbling the ball between my legs and making no-look passes. I wore the same pair of old floppy socks. I even carefully wrote his number on my favorite practice T-shirt with a Magic Marker.

Today, countless sports figures are the heroes of starry-eyed youngsters wanting to emulate their every move and attitude. Sporting goods companies now help those kids to look the part of their heroes. Jackets, shoes, jerseys, hats, sunglasses, and even cologne are part of a megamillion-dollar business that seems to have no end. Everybody wants to be like his favorite superstar athlete.

Who should the Christian athlete look to as an example? Where does he find a model after whom to pattern his performance? The writer of Hebrews tells us that we should "run with endurance the race that God has set before us. We do this by *keeping our eyes on Jesus,* on whom our faith depends from start to finish" (Hebrews 12:1–2 NLT, italics added).

Jesus is the One to watch. He is the One to pattern your life after. He is the perfect role model for every area of life. If Jesus had been an athlete, He would have been the perfect athlete, demonstrating every aspect of real success.

WDJD?

It is common to see wristbands and T-shirts with "WWJD?" or "What would Jesus do?" written on them. The question for our study, however, needs to be, "What *did* Jesus do?" If you want to be the perfect athlete, it is important that you study the life of Jesus closely, because everything about His life is an example for you to follow. What characteristics can be seen in the life of Jesus that demonstrate true success for the Christian athlete?

HE DEMONSTRATED PERSEVERANCE

When I think of former North Carolina State basketball coach Jim Valvano, two things come to mind. The first is a picture of him running onto the court to hug his players when his team won the national championship in 1983. The other is hearing him, in the midst of his battle with cancer, utter his famous statement "Never give up." His courageous fight to the end was inspirational to all who followed his story.

But it was Jesus Christ who demonstrated the "never give up" attitude like no one else who ever lived. He was abandoned by those who loved Him, falsely accused by those who were jealous of Him, horribly tortured by those who made fun of Him, and brutally executed by those who despised Him. Yet, because of His love for you and me, He never quit. The Bible describes it this way,

> He was willing to die a shameful death on the cross because of the joy he knew would be his afterward. Now he is seated in the place of highest honor beside God's throne in heaven. Think about all he endured when sinful people did such terrible things to him, so that you don't become weary and give up. After all, you have not given your lives in your struggle against sin. (HEBREWS 12:2–4 NLT)

All-pro defensive end Reggie White, in his book *In the Trenches,* speaks of perseverance this way:

Don't give up! Don't let anything or anyone stop you. Do what is right and do the work God has given you to do. Very few touchdowns are made with a single 99-yard pass. Most touchdowns come at the end of a ten- or fifteen-down drive made up of five-yard plays, three-yard plays, and even some lost yards.[1]

Jesus' example of endurance should inspire us to endure. It did not matter what came His way; He never gave up. The next time you are tempted to quit, remember Jesus! When you don't think you can make that last line drill, remember Jesus! When you don't think you can make it through the first day of two-a-days, remember Jesus! When you are thirty points down with two minutes to go, remember Jesus! Never give up! Follow His example!

HE WAS NOT DISTRACTED FROM HIS PURPOSE

Every athlete knows the importance of staying focused, of not being distracted from your purpose. I coached a Little League baseball team when my son was younger. It was the first year for the boys to actually pitch in the games. That usually meant a lot of walks and strikeouts. Not too exciting—especially if you played in the outfield. It was not uncommon to look up to see one of the outfielders picking grass or gazing over the fence, watching another game on an adjacent field. Once in a while someone would hit one into the outfield, but it was rarely caught for an out. Why? The outfielders weren't focused on the game.

Jesus was completely focused on His purpose. All of His earthly ministry pointed to the time when He would go to Jerusalem and eventually give His life. Many people were making demands of Him; nevertheless, He stayed focused on His purpose. He knew about the pain and suffering that was ahead for Him. Still, He stayed focused on His purpose. Nothing was more important to Him. Nothing would keep Him from doing what He came to do.

When the days were approaching for His ascension, He was determined to go to Jerusalem; and He sent messengers on ahead of Him, and they went and entered a village of the Samaritans to make

THE RIGHT WAY TO WIN

arrangements for Him. But they did not receive Him, because *He was traveling toward Jerusalem.* (LUKE 9:51–53; emphasis added)

HE UNDERSTOOD THE VALUE OF PREPARATION

Much to the dismay of my wife, I am a huge boxing fan. I love to watch a good fight, and when my hand is on the remote, you can be sure the TV will wind up on a boxing match somewhere on the cable. There is nothing like two fighters, at the peak of their conditioning, slugging it out for all it is worth. However, there is nothing more frustrating to a boxing fan than to see a fighter show up for a match twenty pounds overweight and out of shape. Don't they understand that if they are going to win, they must devote time to preparation? Legendary coach Joe Paterno once said, "The will to win is important, but the will to prepare is vital."

Jesus understood this important truth and demonstrated it in His daily life. Every day of His ministry, He was surrounded by people who needed Him and wanted things from Him. Here is a sample of a typical day as found in the gospel of Mark:

- His day begins with several hours of teaching in the synagogue (1:21–22).
- He is harassed by a man with an evil spirit (1:23–24).
- Jesus casts out the evil spirit (1:25–26).
- He travels to the home of Simon and Andrew (1:29).
- He ministers to Simon's sick mother-in-law and heals her (1:30–31).
- He spends His evening healing great numbers of sick and demon-possessed people who find Him (1:32–34).

Now, I don't know about you, but after a day like that I would have slept in the next morning. Not so with Jesus. He began the next busy day preparing for what He would face. Mark 1:35 records it this way, "Very early in the morning, while it was still dark, Jesus got up, left the house and went off to a solitary place, where he prayed" (NIV). He knew that if He was going to be successful in His busy schedule, He had to prepare.

It is never easy to find the time or the energy to prepare effectively. It was the same for Jesus. But He made preparing a priority. He had to be prepared! Follow His example the next time you feel too tired to get up and work out. Remember His emphasis on preparation when you don't seem to have enough time to shoot those free throws.

HE MODELED HUMILITY

You may not know the name Joe DeLoach. He is the only man to ever beat Carl Lewis in an Olympic final. And he did it in dramatic fashion, winning the gold medal and setting the world record in the 200 meters. I spoke with Joe and asked him what characteristic of Jesus most inspired him as an athlete. His answer was, "The humility of Jesus." He told me that, because of his own accomplishments, he constantly needed to be reminded not to be too big for his britches, to stay humble.

Although there is nothing wrong with enjoying victory, it is important to remember to give glory to the One who has blessed you with your abilities. Be aware that you are never too "big time" to encourage a younger athlete or sign an autograph. You are only as good as the talent you have been blessed with.

Jesus Christ didn't take into account His "big time" status as the Son of God, when He gave up His position to come to earth as a man and sacrifice His life for us. The Bible explains:

> Your attitude should be the same that Christ Jesus had. Though he was God, he did not demand and cling to his rights as God. He made himself nothing; he took the humble position of a slave and appeared in human form. And in human form he obediently humbled himself even further by dying a criminal's death on a cross. (PHILIPPIANS 2:5–8 NLT)

HE HAD DISCIPLINE

Someone has defined discipline as doing what you have to do whether you feel like it or not. Every athlete worth his or her salt understands that kind of attitude. It's going out to run alone early in the morning when you would rather sleep a little longer. It's shooting free throws one after another, long after practice has ended. It's taking swings in the batting cage until your arms ache. Discipline—it is the characteristic that separates the wanna-bes from the gonna-bes.

THE RIGHT WAY TO WIN

Jesus modeled discipline constantly in His earthly life. He knew His purpose on earth was to give His life as a sacrifice—to die a painful, horrible death on a cross. He didn't want to go through with it, but He did anyway. The night He was arrested in the Garden of Gethsemene, He prayed, "My Father, if it is possible, may this cup be taken from me. Yet not as I will, but as you will" (Matthew 26:39 NIV).

Jesus did what He had to do whether He felt like it or not. He knew what He faced was extremely difficult, but He did it anyway. That's discipline that leads to real success. What an example for you to follow!

HE HELPED MAKE OTHERS BETTER

Anyone who is a leader on his team is concerned with making his or her teammates better. In 1970, Willis Reed was Mr. Everything in the NBA. He was the MVP in the all-star game and for the league. But nowhere was his influence felt as strongly that year as it was for the New York Knicks in the championship finals, where he also won the MVP award.

The finals pitted the Los Angeles Lakers against the Knicks, and it was one of the most memorable play-offs ever. The series was tied two games apiece going into game five. The Knicks pulled out the fifth game, but they lost Reed, their star center, to a severe muscle tear. Without him, the Knicks were trounced by the Lakers and *their* star center, Wilt Chamberlain, in the sixth game. With the seventh and deciding game left, the big question was whether Reed would be able to play.

Shortly before the start of the game, Reed hobbled out onto the floor, dressed to play, sending the crowd to their feet and firing up the Knicks players. Despite being in severe pain, he played the first half, inspiring his teammates and leading New York to the championship. There was something about Willis Reed's being on the floor and giving his all that made his teammates better competitors. Some players just seem to have that ability.

Jesus Christ made everyone around Him better. He took an odd assortment of men from different backgrounds and made a difference in and through them. Some were fishermen, some tax collectors, some educated, and others apparently without any schooling, but because of the influence of Jesus Christ they became men who literally changed the world.

Simon Peter was one of those men. When his brother brought him to meet Jesus, he was simply an uneducated, untrained, hard-living fisherman. Jesus took one look at him and saw beyond his rough edges. When Jesus looked at Simon the fisherman, he saw Cephas the rock. He saw his potential and spent the next three years helping Simon Peter be all he could be.

Looking intently at Simon, Jesus said, "You *are* Simon son of John. You *will* be called Cephas [rock]" (John 1:42 NIV, emphasis added).

HE KEPT THE PROPER PERSPECTIVE

Another characteristic of Jesus that is important to observe is His perspective. He lived His life in a way that clearly demonstrated His priorities. His outlook was spiritual, and it was eternal. He never allowed anyone or anything to change that perspective.

One day Jesus was speaking to a large group of folks inside a house. In fact, the house was so packed that there was no room for anyone else.

And then four guys showed up carrying a friend who was paralyzed. They wanted to see Jesus, hoping He would heal their friend, but they couldn't even get close to the front door. They were so determined to see their friend healed that they climbed onto the roof, removed a section of it, and lowered the man to the floor in front of Jesus. Jesus looked at the paralyzed man and said, "Son, your sins are forgiven" (Mark 2:5).

Now I would expect that the man's four friends were more than a little disappointed at those words. They were hoping for a healing instead of a spiritual cleansing. And Jesus did finally heal the man, but not before He dealt with the spiritual side of things. Jesus was looking at things from a different perspective. He knew that the priority was spiritual, not physical.

I have a friend who played football for the Naval Academy. He told me that when he looks at the life of Jesus, it reminds him that life is bigger than the game. It helps him to keep in mind that his purpose for playing football is to glorify God. Do you know what is most important? Do you have the proper perspective? Follow the example of Jesus.

HE GAVE HIS ALL

I won't tell you how many times I have watched the film *The Natural*. Actually, I lost count a long time ago. No matter how many times I have seen it, though, it still gives me goose bumps to watch Roy Hobbs, played by Robert Redford, hit the game-winning home run into the lights to lead his team to victory. There is something incredibly inspiring about watching him as he stands at the plate, blood on his jersey, somehow reaching down deep to give his all.

We have already discussed the importance of giving your all. It is a trademark quality of every great athlete. However, nowhere is a 150-percent performance seen in a greater way than through the life and death of Jesus Christ. There have been times when we all have hurt and ached and struggled, but our experiences have never even come close to the total commitment He gave for us.

> He was despised and rejected—a man of sorrows, acquainted with bitterest grief. We turned our backs on him and looked the other way when he went by. He was despised, and we did not care. Yet it was our weaknesses he carried; it was our sorrows that weighed him down. And we thought his troubles were a punishment from God for his own sins! But he was wounded and crushed for our sins. He was beaten that we might have peace. He was whipped, and we were healed! All of us have strayed away like sheep. We have left God's paths to follow our own. Yet the Lord laid on him the guilt and sins of us all. (ISAIAH 53:3–6 NLT)

Learn from the example of Jesus. Never has anyone else demonstrated every characteristic necessary to experience true success. But He did it all, and He will help you to be all you need to be—as an athlete and, most important, as a person. Keep your eyes on Him!

> I can do everything through him who gives me strength. (PHILIPPIANS 4:13 NIV)

74

To Think About

1. Who are some of your sports heroes?

2. In what ways can these heroes fall short of being proper role models?

3. Which of these characteristics from the life of Jesus do you most need to apply to your own life?

   Perseverance

   Focused on the purpose

   Prepared for the task

   Humility

   Discipline

   Helping others to be better

   Keeping the proper perspective

   Giving 100 percent

4. What specific steps can you take to help you improve in these areas?

7

DEALING WITH PRESSURE

Pressure. It's a way of life in our society today. A recent study indicated that more than 30,000,000,000 aspirins are taken in the United States each year. That's a lot of headaches!

These tensions are no stranger to the athlete. There is the pressure to win, the pressure to make the team, the pressure to keep your position, and the pressures that go with dealing with criticism, to name a few.

There are also the many pressures that are unique to the Christian athlete. A survey of the twenty finalists for Christian Athlete of the Year in the state of Texas revealed the greatest pressures they face. Here are some of the responses:

- To be the best you can be
- To measure up to non-Christian athletes
- Standing alone as a Christian
- Trying not to blow your witness with your teammates
- The temptation to please others instead of Christ
- Being consistent in your relationship with the Lord

- Living up to the expectations of others
- Keeping the Lord first in your life
- Spending enough time reading your Bible
- Dealing with the ungodly atmosphere in the locker room
- Always being positive and upbeat
- Knowing people are constantly watching you

You will face two types of pressure as an athlete. One type of pressure is the kind over which you have control. This is usually the pressure that comes because you have failed to prepare properly. It's showing up out of shape for the first day of practice. It's going into a competition without a plan or without proper research.

I have a recurring nightmare that I am supposed to take a final exam for a class and I realize I haven't studied. In fact, I don't even have a book. And to top it off, I can't remember where the classroom is because I haven't been there all semester. Although it is just a nightmare, it represents pressure that comes from a lack of preparation.

We have already dealt with the issue of wholehearted preparation, so I won't overdo it. But it is important to realize that some pressures you face *can* be eliminated by just being better prepared. The more prepared you are, the less pressure you will experience.

Another type of pressure, however, is the kind that is unavoidable. It is beyond the realm of your control. This kind of pressure usually comes from outside sources. It is the pressure to win that comes from the coach or the media. It is also the pressure to live up to someone else's expectations. This is the kind of pressure you must learn to face, because there is nothing you can do to prevent it.

The most important issue to consider about pressure is how you are going to deal with it. It's there, and it won't go away. The coach won't let it, and neither will the fans. You can't run from it; you can't pretend it's not there; you must face it.

Legendary basketball coach John Wooden says:

If you are trying to live up to expectations put on you by the media, parents, fans, your employer, or whatever else there may be, it's going to af-

fect you adversely because it brings on worry and anxiety. I think that is the tendency of people who choke under pressure. They're thinking about living up to the expectations of everybody else instead of just doing their job the best they can.[1]

So how can you deal with pressure? Several principles found in God's Word will help you cope with the stresses and pressures you face as an athlete.

The first principle is to *look to God's promises.* Whatever you are up against, there is no greater source of comfort, hope, and relief than the Scriptures.

Such things were written in the Scriptures long ago to teach us. They give us hope and encouragement as we wait patiently for God's promises. (ROMANS 15:4 NLT)

Billie Winsett, All Big-Eight outside hitter and on the 1995 Nebraska national champion women's volleyball team, explains how she was able to cope with the pressure of a championship drive. She says:

The way I got rid of the pressure was seeking God and seeking His plan. I went through a concordance trying to find verses for whatever I needed that night, because it was very stressful. . . . Psalm 118 relaxes me in the sense that I can just relax and play. I don't have to worry about the pressures within the coliseum—from my coach, my teammates' expectations or even my own. I just have to play my best and that's all that God requires of me.[2]

Rely on encouragement from the Scriptures to get you through the tough spots. God's Word will help you in every area. Memorize some passages that you find helpful in your situation. Here are a few that will encourage you:

I can do all things through Him who strengthens me. (PHILIPPIANS 4:13)

He who dwells in the shelter of the Most High will abide in the shadow of the Almighty. (PSALM 91:1)

My soul waits in silence for God only; from Him is my salvation. He only is my rock and my salvation, my stronghold; I shall not be greatly shaken. (PSALM 62:1–2)

God is our refuge and strength, a very present help in trouble. Therefore we will not fear, though the earth should change and though the mountains slip into the heart of the sea. (PSALM 46:1–2)

I will lift up my eyes to the mountains; from whence shall my help come? My help comes from the Lord, who made heaven and earth. (PSALM 121:1–2)

The second guideline you should follow is to *pray for God's perspective*. In other words, you need to ask the Lord to help you see your situation through His eyes. The view that God sees is far better than the view you can see.

The prophet Elisha and his followers faced some pressures when the Arameans came after them. They awoke one morning to find the entire city surrounded by the army of the king of Aram. Talk about pressure. There were chariots, horses, and soldiers everywhere.

One of Elisha's servants was really feeling the stress, and he began to buckle under the pressure. The Bible records:

"Ah, my lord, what will we do now?" he cried out to Elisha. "Don't be afraid!" Elisha told him. "For there are more on our side than on theirs!" Then Elisha prayed, "O Lord, open his eyes and let him see!" The Lord opened his servant's eyes, and when he looked up, he saw that the hillside around Elisha was filled with horses and chariots of fire. (2 KINGS 6:15–17 NLT)

Once the servant was able to view things from God's perspective, he was able to see that God had His army of angels protecting Elisha. Ask God to help you see things the way He sees them.

So we don't look at the troubles we can see right now; rather, we look forward to what we have not yet seen. For the troubles we see will soon be over, but the joys to come will last forever. (2 CORINTHI-ANS 4:18 NLT)

The third important principle to follow when dealing with pressure is to *surrender to the awesome ability of God.* He is bigger than any pressure you face, and nothing takes Him by surprise. You must let His power work through you.

By his mighty power at work within us, he is able to accomplish infinitely more than we would ever dare to ask or hope. (EPHESIANS 3:20 NLT)

This truth is demonstrated throughout the Bible in the lives of people God has used. One example is Samson. I really don't think Samson looked like a champion bodybuilder. Now, I know the movies always show him as a musclebound hulk of a specimen, but the Bible paints a different picture. You see, everyone was always trying to find out the source of his strength.

So Delilah said to Samson, "Tell me the secret of your great strength and how you can be tied up and subdued." (JUDGES 16:6 NIV)

If Samson had looked as though he'd spent most of his life in the weight room, no one would have ever been curious as to why he was so strong. It would have been obvious. Instead, everyone kept asking what the source of his strength was.

The truth is that Samson probably looked fairly average. Maybe he was shaped like me. It really didn't matter. The true source of his strength was God.

Then Samson called to the Lord and said, "O Lord God, please remember me and please strengthen me just this time." (JUDGES 16:28)

His strength was found in the fact that God was strong through him. That is the principle you must follow in the midst of pressure. Let God be strong through you. Allow His awesome ability to do its work in your life.

For the eyes of the Lord move to and fro throughout the earth that He may strongly support those whose heart is completely His. (2 CHRONICLES 16:9)

The fourth principle is to *rest in His presence.* The Bible speaks often of the need to rest in the Lord. It is a concept we must understand, because there is a tremendous relief from all pressures that comes from resting in the Lord.

Now, some of you might be saying, "I rest in the Lord every time the pastor preaches a long sermon, and I hope no one hears me snoring!" Actually, that's not it. Resting in the Lord is taking worries, stresses, pressures—all the things that are weighing you down—and giving them to Him. I once heard it said, "Every night when I go to bed, I give all my worries to God. He's going to be up all night anyway." The Bible says it this way:

> Be still in the presence of the Lord, and wait patiently for him to act. (PSALM 37:7 NLT)

> Don't worry about anything; instead, pray about everything. Tell God what you need, and thank him for all he has done. If you do this, you will experience God's peace, which is far more wonderful than the human mind can understand. His peace will guard your hearts and minds as you live in Christ Jesus. (PHILIPPIANS 4:6–7 NLT)

> Cast all your anxiety on [God] because he cares for you. (1 PETER 5:7 NIV)

The apostle Paul understood both pressure and the need to trust in God to take care of it. He writes:

> I think you ought to know, dear brothers and sisters, about the trouble we went through in the province of Asia. We were crushed and completely overwhelmed, and we thought we would never live through it. In fact, we expected to die. But as a result, we learned not to rely on ourselves, but on God who can raise the dead. And he did deliver us from mortal danger. And we are confident that he will continue to deliver us. (2 CORINTHIANS 1:8–10 NLT)

Learn to rest in the Lord. Perhaps it will help you to meditate on a passage of Scripture or listen to praise music when you begin to feel pressures weighing you down. Whatever works best for you, turn it all over to Him. He can handle it!

The fifth principle to help you deal with pressure is to *focus on your priorities.* There's a wonderful commercial that is an advertisement for March Madness Basketball. It's the one where a boy is concentrating on shooting a free throw while his friend is doing everything he can do to distract him. He waves balloons, wears a rainbow wig, shoots an air horn, screams at the top of his lungs, and even unrolls a poster of a girl in a bikini. All the while, the young man at the free-throw line focuses on the rim, takes the shot, and hits nothing but net. What a great picture of focus and concentration!

One of the best things you can do to help you face pressure is to concentrate on your priorities. As we have already discussed, your number one priority as a Christian athlete is to please the only fan in the stands—Jesus Christ. Keep your eyes on Him. Determine to please Him above all else and focus wholeheartedly on that priority.

I visited with a Christian woman who plays volleyball at the University of Oklahoma. She said the greatest pressure she faces on a regular basis is the pressure to be the best. I asked her how she deals with that pressure, and her response showed wonderful maturity. She said, "God doesn't ask you to be the best—He just asks you to be *your* best."

Keep your eyes on Jesus, the only fan in the stands. Focus your all on pleasing Him. The pressures will come, but they will not distract you if you keep your eyes on Him.

To Think About

1. List some of the pressures you struggle with as an athlete.

2. Which of these pressures can you change? Are any of them present because you have failed to do something? If so, determine the actions you need to take to remove that pressure.

3. The rest of the pressures on your list are things you cannot control. Ask yourself the following questions about them:

   • Is there a passage of Scripture that will help me to view this pressure in a different light?

   • How difficult is this pressure from God's perspective?

Have I surrendered this to the Lord? What can I focus on that will keep me from focusing on this pressure?

8

HANDLING SETBACKS

It was 1973. The Baylor University football team was in its second year under head coach Grant Teaff. The young team had struggled through most of the season and now found itself facing Texas Christian University for the Baylor homecoming game. Behind 34–7 at the start of the fourth quarter, quarterback Neal Jeffrey led his team to score three touchdowns before the home crowd and bring the score to 34–28 with just minutes to go in the game.

After stopping TCU, Baylor took over the ball for one final drive. Jeffrey masterfully moved his team down to the 12-yard line, and with the clock running down, Coach Teaff called his last time-out to set up what would hopefully be the winning score. Neal hit the tailback with a short pass on the next play, but the player was tackled inbounds short of the goal line. With no time-outs left, Jeffrey quickly threw the ball out-of-bounds in an effort to stop the clock. What he didn't realize was that it was fourth down. TCU took over the ball, ran the clock out, and won the game 34–28. The young quarterback's mistake cost Baylor the game.

How did Neal Jeffrey choose to deal with this setback? First of all, he realized that life is bigger than one mistake in one game. He knew that was true because of his faith in Jesus Christ. Second, he knew God could use this embarrassing and painful moment to build character and accomplish great things in his life. Neal Jeffrey experienced true success in the midst of difficulty. The following year he led the Baylor Bears to the Cotton Bowl and the Southwest Conference championship before spending several years in the NFL.

How does the Christian athlete experience success in the midst of setbacks? You may get cut from your team or perhaps get injured and lose your starting spot. How do you deal with such difficulties? And why do they happen?

CAUSES FOR STRUGGLES AND DIFFICULTIES

The Bible says there are several causes for difficulties and struggles in our lives. Some are our fault, and others are out of our control.

First, the Bible indicates that *some difficulties come as a result of our own disobedience.* King David experienced huge problems in his life as a direct result of sin. It had been his choice to sin, and he knew there were consequences to pay. He wrote to God:

> For I recognize my shameful deeds—they haunt me day and night. Against you, and you alone, have I sinned; I have done what is evil in your sight. You will be proved right in what you say, and your judgment against me is just. (PSALM 51:3–4 NLT)

In an article in *Sports Illustrated* about a year before Mickey Mantle died, he discussed his battle with alcoholism. He said:

> *I can admit that all of the drinking shortened my career. . . . God gave me a great body to play with, and I didn't take care of it. And I blame a lot of it on alcohol.*[1]

Some problems and difficulties that you experience are simply consequences of things you do. They are not the result of bad luck or divine punishment. They exist because of poor choices and bad decisions. The Bible makes that clear when it says, "A man reaps what he sows" (Galatians 6:7 NIV).

Second, *some difficulties come as a result of sin and disobedience in the lives of others.* The fact is that there those who are innocent victims and suffer because of others and their sins. Whether it be the family that loses a child at the hands of a drunk driver or the physically impaired baby born to a drug-addicted mother, the plain fact is that we live in an evil world surrounded by evil people, and sometimes there are innocent victims. I do not understand it, and I cannot explain it, but I know it happens.

Third, *some difficulties come specifically so that God might receive glory.* Some struggles and difficulties happen in the life of a Christian that ultimately lead to other people's seeing the greatness of God. For example, during the ministry of Jesus, a man named Lazarus became sick:

> He lived in Bethany with his sisters, Mary and Martha. This is the Mary who poured the expensive perfume on the Lord's feet and wiped them with her hair. Her brother, Lazarus, was sick. So the two sisters sent a message to Jesus telling him, "Lord, the one you love is very sick." But when Jesus heard about it he said, "Lazarus's sickness will not end in death. No, it is for the glory of God. I, the Son of God, will receive glory from this." (JOHN 11:1–4 NLT)

Ultimately, the Lord raised Lazarus from the dead, and many people saw the power of God. The glory went to the Lord.

Jim Ryun had won just about every honor and award a runner could win except a gold medal in the Olympics. The year was 1972, and it seemed to be the time he would accomplish the feat that had eluded him. Going into the competition in Munich, he was the hands-down favorite to win the gold. But tragedy struck during the race of his life. With less than 500 meters to go, he was tripped by another runner and fell, spraining his ankle and ending his chances for the prized Olympic gold medal.

A number of years later, he would experience real success from his difficult Olympic experience. He writes:

> *Since running had been my one and only god, in order to give me something far better and more enduring, He had to take my substitute god away.*

Thus I grew to a point of genuine thankfulness for what happened that day on the Munich track in 1972. For out of the dust of defeat blossomed the new life that came to flourish in my heart. Finally, I am always quick to recall the words of my Swedish friend, "God will use the fall for His glory," and I realize He has done precisely that.[2]

Some difficulties come expressly that we might grow. I do not profess to understand all that is involved here, but the Scripture is clear—God allows struggles in our lives and uses them to grow us spiritually.

Consider it all joy, my brethren, when you encounter various trials, knowing that *the testing of your faith produces endurance.* And let endurance have its perfect result, so *that you may be perfect and complete, lacking in nothing.* (JAMES 1:2–4, emphasis added)

Knowing that God has your best interest in mind may not make things any easier, but it does help you to see an ultimate benefit. This concept should be easier to understand for an athlete than for anyone else. An athlete knows well the pain and difficulty that come with preparation. Hours in the weight room, running line drills, and two-a-days are examples of what is not always enjoyable about being an athlete. But even though it hurts and it is not fun, you know it will all ultimately benefit you in your performance.

That's the way it is for a Christian going through struggles. Although they are painful and not any fun at all, you know they will ultimately benefit you in your spiritual life. That is God's promise. He will take whatever difficulty you go through and use it for your growth and your good.

And we know that God causes all things to work together for good to those who love God, to those who are called according to His purpose. (ROMANS 8:28)

Legendary broadcaster Ernie Harwell, speaking on facing difficulty, said:

It feels like a football game or a baseball game. I know what the final score is going to be. The ups and downs throughout the game are something that I don't really have a lot of control over. I try to do the best I can. God has got a plan for me. Whatever that plan is, it is good because He loves me.[3]

If you are going to grow and experience God's presence in the middle of difficulty, there are two words you must learn to relate to. They are *perspective* and *trust*. These are the essentials to true success when facing setbacks.

A PROPER PERSPECTIVE

My all-time favorite movie is *Jeremiah Johnson*. It's the story of a young man who heads off to the mountains to become a mountain man. He tells of all his experiences along the way. After a difficult start, young Jeremiah meets up with a veteran mountain man named Bear Claw. Bear Claw takes him under his wing and teaches him all he needs to know to survive in the mountains before sending him out on his own.

Over a period of time, Johnson has a wife and a child, only to see them killed in a long-running battle with a group of Indians. He is forced to fight for his life many times and winds up with numerous scars from battles he has endured.

Near the end of the picture, he is reunited with his old friend Bear Claw. As they sit down to a meal, Bear Claw looks at Jeremiah and says, "You've come far, pilgrim." Jeremiah, stretching and feeling the pain of many injuries and difficulties, says, "Feels like far." "Were it worth the trouble?" says Bear Claw. Jeremiah responds, "What trouble?"

I love that scene because it pictures an important truth about difficulty for Christians—it's all about perspective. It is realizing that trouble may not really be trouble in the long run. It may be God molding and shaping you. It may be an important part of God's making you into everything He wants you to be.

LEARNING TO TRUST

Developing the right perspective really boils down to one issue: trusting God. Are you willing to trust Him, believing that He is big enough to understand your difficulties, even though *you* don't understand?

> Trust in the Lord with all your heart and do not lean on your own understanding. (PROVERBS 3:5)

> A man's steps are directed by the Lord. (PROVERBS 20:24 NIV)

How do you learn to trust? Where do you start? The best illustration involves flying on an airplane. Just look around the next time you fly. You can always tell the people who have never flown before. They are the ones who are listening intently to the stewardess explain how to fasten the seat belt and what to do in the event of cabin depressurization. They carefully read the flight information card "located in the seat pocket in front of you." The people who fly all the time are reading, sleeping, or gazing into oblivion.

I recently sat by a woman who was flying for the first time. She was a nervous wreck. Every time there was an interesting noise such as the landing gear being raised, she would scream. When we made that initial bump of touching down on the runway during landing, she was so nervous that she missed the armrest and put a death grip on my knee that Mr. Spock would envy.

I followed her off the plane and watched as her family met her in the terminal. I couldn't help but laugh as I overheard her explaining to them how flying was a breeze and there was nothing to it.

What had happened? Her first completed experience of flying had taught her that it wasn't as bad as she had feared. The return flight was probably much more relaxed for her—not to mention for whomever sat next to her. And if she's flown a few more times, by now she's probably snoozing while the stewardess gives her speech.

Trusting God is a lot like flying on an airplane. The more you trust Him, the more you learn that He is worthy of your trust. The more you learn He is worthy of your trust, the more you trust Him. Trusting God is a lifelong process.

The dictionary defines trust as "putting someone confidently in charge of something." Trusting God in the midst of difficulty is exercising faith in the fact that He is in charge and He is capable of being in charge, whether we understand things or not.

The first time I remember learning about trusting God in difficulty was through the lives of a couple of friends, Ray and Judy Hildebrand. You may not recognize the name Ray Hildebrand, but Ray was the Paul of Paul and Paula, a duo that had several hit records in the early 60s. We became friends when Ray was working for the Fellowship of Christian Athletes. He was a great help to me my first couple of years in college, and because of his recommendation I had a number of opportunities to speak and sing at various places around the country.

One morning, shortly after Ray had left for work, a man trying to break into their house shot Judy. The authorities called Ray at work, and he hurried to the hospital. When he arrived, the doctors told him they didn't know whether his wife would survive or not.

After hearing that report, Ray sat down in a corner of the waiting room, and while he waited he began writing a song called "He's Been Wonderful to Me." The song tells of God's goodness, and the very last line says, "I'm learning I can trust Him, the one who lives in my heart."

Judy ultimately recovered from her wounds, but I never recovered from the message of the song. You see, I'd discovered something. Ray didn't learn that day in the hospital that he could trust God to make Judy OK. No, he learned he could trust God whether Judy recovered or not. That was the message of the song. You can trust God! No matter what happens—you can trust Him.

I discovered that every difficulty, every setback, every struggle is an opportunity to trust God. Whatever trouble you face in your life, it is an opportunity for you to trust Him. It was that lesson learned from Ray and Judy that helped me to trust the Lord through very difficult times in my own life years later.

Professional golfer Paul Azinger in his book *Zinger* discusses how he came to deal with the news that he had cancer and how it impacted his relationship with God. He says:

When things happen to us that we don't understand, we can scream, "Why me? Why me, God?" We can allow circumstances to drive us away from God. Or we can do an about-face and run to God and cling to Him and find in Him our security and our hope. I decided I wanted to run to God, and that's what I did. . . . I decided that I was going to trust Jesus Christ, not only in this struggle against cancer, but with my life, all my life, completely, for as long—or as short—a time as He gave me.[4]

The bottom line is, you will surely experience difficulty in your life. It may be small, or it may be large. The important thing is how you choose to view it and how you choose to face it. Learn to trust the Lord! Trusting Him will give you a perspective on your difficulties that will allow you to be all God wants you to be. Trusting Him through trouble will bring you real success.

Those who trust in the Lord are [as secure] as Mount Zion, which cannot be moved but abides forever. (PSALM 125:1)

To Think About

1. What are some setbacks in your athletic career that you have experienced personally?

2. What benefits have you been able to see coming from those difficulties?

3. Have you grown closer to the Lord as a result of the difficulties?

4. In what areas of life do you need to trust the Lord more?

9

IMPACTING YOUR TEAMMATES

**LIVE WISELY AMONG
THOSE WHO ARE NOT
CHRISTIANS, AND
MAKE THE MOST OF
EVERY OPPORTUNITY.**

(COLOSSIANS 4:5 NLT)

Jay plays baseball at a major university. He is a starter and has been for two years. One of his greatest concerns is to make a difference for the Lord in the lives of his teammates. However, it is the "team thing" to go out drinking and partying. So Jay struggles with balancing being a part of the team but not being a part of everything his teammates do. It bothers him to regularly hear the Lord's name taken in vain on and off the field. But he's not sure whether to say so and risk a damaged relationship with a teammate or to just keep his mouth closed and tough it out. He wants to reach them, not push them away.

While researching the material for this book, I talked with several hundred high school, college, and professional athletes. Almost without exception, every Christian athlete I interviewed said his greatest struggle is how to effectively make an impact on his teammates. How do you witness to those you know best and those who know you best? What are some ways you can have an eternal impact on your teammates?

BE UNDERSTANDING

First, it is important to keep in mind that you can't expect people who aren't Christians to act like Christians. So don't be upset at teammates who swear and act inappropriately. They don't know any better. Don't be surprised and offended by the horrible behavior you see in the lives of non-Christian teammates. It may be the best they can do. Don't expect them to live by the same standards you do.

I remember the close of one particular chapel service held for the Royals. One of the players stayed around after everyone else had left. He asked me to sing again the song I had sung to end the service. We went back into our meeting room, and I sang it for him. After I was finished, he looked at me with tears in his eyes and said, "*#@*! That really got to me!" Now, I could have been upset or even offended, but I knew he was speaking straight from his heart. He didn't intend any disrespect; he just didn't know any better.

One of the first things you have to do, if you are to be a witness to your non-Christian teammates, is to look past what they do and see what they are. They are lost, and they desperately need Jesus Christ! Don't let their attitudes and actions get in the way. See them the way Jesus sees them. Look at their hearts.

> Seeing the people, He felt compassion for them, because they were distressed and dispirited like sheep without a shepherd. (MATTHEW 9:36)

BE REAL

I knew a high-profile professional athlete who was the chapel leader for his team. The problem was that he was always too busy to come to chapel himself. He liked the title of "Chapel Leader," but his relationship with God was low on his priority list. The other players heard him talk a spiritual talk but saw him live his life in a completely different manner. In the long run, he had a negative impact on his teammates, because they saw him for what he really was, not for what he said he was.

If you are going to make an impact for Christ on your teammates, you can't pretend to be something you are not. In the long run, you will have no effective impact at all. Your strongest witness to them is what they see, not what you say.

It is like the story of the duck who claimed to be a dog. It didn't matter what he said, and it didn't matter how much he hung out with the dogs. As long as he looked like a duck, quacked like a duck, walked like a duck, and ate duck food, he was a duck. Whether it was clear to him or not, it was obvious to both the other ducks and the dogs.

You cannot claim to be a Christian and expect to have a witness with your teammates if you don't act like a Christian. The Bible says a Christian is a new person. If you want to make an impact for Christ, you must understand your responsibility to live in a Christlike manner. You have a responsibility to be different.

> Those who become Christians become new persons. They are not the same anymore, for the old life is gone. A new life has begun! (2 CORINTHIANS 5:17 NLT)

BE CONSISTENT

Dave played ball for me back in my coaching days. He had become a Christian when he was in high school, but he had strayed from the Lord and was living his life in the fast lane. He stopped by my office to see me one day, quite concerned about a friend of his. This friend was a teammate on his city league softball team. He had just gotten the news he had terminal cancer and had a very short time to live.

Dave wanted me to go by the hospital to see his friend, because he didn't think he was a Christian. He really wanted to go as well, but he thought his friend would be shocked to learn he was a Christian because of the way he had lived his life in front of him. He didn't want his poor example to hinder his teammate in this critical decision.

The young man in the hospital trusted Christ as his Savior and died the next day. How tragic that Dave was unable to tell his teammate about the most important thing in life because of the behavior he had demonstrated.

If you are going to have a positive impact on your teammates, it is imperative that you model the Christian life. You can't expect to live any way you want and be able to make a difference in a teammate's life when it really counts.

> You were formerly darkness, but now you are Light in the Lord; walk as children of Light. (EPHESIANS 5:8)

BE AVAILABLE

I had invested a fair amount of time building a relationship with one of the ballplayers on the Royals who was not a Christian. He liked to read, so I often shared with him books about spiritual subjects. We talked regularly, and he would occasionally come to chapel service.

One Saturday night, he and his wife were out with some friends when they were robbed at gunpoint. My friend was attempting to wrestle the weapon away from the robber when the gun went off, killing the young attacker.

The player arrived at the ballpark the next morning obviously distressed over the previous evening's incident. He checked in with the manager, got excused from the game, and headed straight to find me. As it happened, I had someone with me who led that morning's chapel while I spent a couple of hours with this ballplayer as he faced a time of major crisis.

Sometimes one of the most important and most effective things you can do for your teammates is simply to be available during a time of difficulty. Watch for those times of need in their lives. It might be the death of a relative or something as simple as a minor injury. Your presence and availability can make all the difference in the world.

Be there for your teammates when they are hurting or struggling. Encourage them. God will use you to show His love for them.

BE PREPARED

When I was a Scout, I learned the Scout's motto, *Be Prepared!* Every good Scout knew the importance of taking everything he needed on an overnight camp out. If you are going to be an effective witness to your teammates, you must follow the same philosophy. Be a prepared witness! "Always be prepared to give an answer to everyone who asks you to give the reason for the hope that you have" (1 Peter 3:15 NIV).

In other words, if you are not sure what to say to someone who wants to become a Christian—*learn*. Many studies and excellent resources are available that will help you to be better prepared to explain your faith. There are also some very simple approaches you can work on that will help you to be effective.

Use your testimony. The easiest thing to explain to someone is your own experience. You don't have to read a book or take a class to know what to say—it's about what happened to you. Just tell your story in your own words.

Keep it simple. Begin by telling what your life was like before you met Christ. Next, tell a little about how you gave your life to Him. Then take a couple of minutes to explain how He has made a difference in your life. This simple approach is easy to use, and no one can argue with your personal experience.

Use a tract. There are many good and very simple leaflets that will help you communicate a clear and concise presentation of the gospel message. You can find them at any Christian bookstore. My favorite is *Steps to Peace with God*, by Billy Graham. I like to use it because people are usually open to read something written by him. Find a tract you are comfortable with, and keep a few with you at all times.

Use the Bible. You can easily take your Bible and mark the verses you want to use in presenting the gospel to someone. Write in the margin the page number of the next verse you want to use and then repeat the process until you have covered the verses you plan using. Write some notes in the margin as well—notes that will help you in your presentation. As you become more familiar with using these verses, you may want to memorize them.

BE DELIBERATE

Joe Aldrich wrote a terrific book about being a witness. It's entitled *Gentle Persuasion*. The opening chapter is called "Can You Bake a Cherry Pie?" The whole point of the chapter is about the simple witnessing tool of giving things to people. A teammate who might not want to talk to you about the Lord may read a good Christian book you give to him. Others, who wouldn't come to church with you, might listen to a tape of a sermon that touches a particular need in their lives.

I have a friend, a well-known professional athlete, whom I have tried to witness to over a period of several years. Every time I see him, I give him something. I have given him books, tapes, and music. I have even given Bibles to each of his children. Although he has never given his life to Christ, I am confident that God is still working on him and using those gifts to plant seeds in his life. I don't know whether he reads all the books or listens to all the tapes, but he always takes them when I give them to him.

Give things to your teammates that will plant seeds in their lives. Invite them to go with you to Christian concerts or special programs that might be of interest to them. Bake them a cherry pie. God will bless those deliberate witnessing opportunities.

BE PATIENT

I was thrilled when I discovered that evangelist Billy Graham, in town for a precrusade meeting, was available to speak at a special chapel service for the Royals and White Sox at the stadium. We gathered for an afternoon meeting, and Dr. Graham, along with Cliff Barrows and Bev Shea, showed up to address a crowd of around fifty people, including a number of ballplayers from both teams.

After a wonderful time of music and testimony followed by a dynamic evangelistic message from Dr. Graham, several people, including some of the players, trusted in Christ as their Savior. It was exciting, because several guys I had been praying for came to know Christ. On the other hand, others listened to the greatest evangelist of our time and did not respond. What's more, some who were invited to the service didn't even show up to hear Billy Graham.

It is important for you to understand that some of your teammates won't be interested in the gospel regardless of what you say or do. It won't matter if Billy Graham himself preaches the gospel to them. Don't be discouraged if your whole team fails to fall on their knees and repent the first time you try to be a witness. Sometimes it takes a while. Be patient!

I first met Clint Hurdle his rookie year as a Kansas City Royal. Before he ever played a game in a major league uniform, he had his picture on the cover of *Sports Illustrated.* He was supposed to be the next Mickey Mantle, a giant superstar. He was everyone's pick for the Hall of Fame as a first-year ballplayer. All this was an enormous amount of pressure for a young athlete. That pressure coupled with his newfound fame was more than he could handle. Life in the fast lane took its toll on Clint Hurdle the athlete and Clint Hurdle the person.

Because we were close in age, we became casual friends while he was with the Royals, and I tried to take advantage of any opportunity I had to tell him of Christ. He was a regular attender at my chapel services, although clearly he was not willing to surrender his life to the Lord.

After he left the Royals, I lost track of Clint, but I continued to pray for him. Several years later, as I was watching television, I heard the announcer for a Christian talk show say, "Coming up next, New York Mets catcher, Clint Hurdle." You can imagine my surprise as I watched Clint tell how he and his wife had recently become Christians.

I sat down and wrote him a letter, expressing my joy at what God had done in his life. Shortly after, I received a reply from him. He wrote:

> *Thanks so much for your encouraging letter. The seeds you planted in Kansas City came to fruit three years ago in Phoenix where my wife and I were saved. Praise God for your faithfulness in sharing His Word. I think of your time spent in chapel in K.C. and pray that my witness will glorify Him.*

God only used me to plant some seeds in Clint Hurdle's life. Later down the road, He used someone else to bring him to Christ. The point is this: It is your responsibility to be a witness to your teammates. But you are not responsible for their response. As in Clint's case, it may take many years and many other people before some of them respond. I have been praying for some of those guys

THE RIGHT WAY TO WIN

from the Royals for more than twenty years, and I still believe they will eventually come to Christ. You just do your part and be patient!

BE PRAYERFUL

Ultimately, one of the most effective things you can do is to pray for your teammates. When all is said or done, it's not about words, convincing arguments, or how many opportunities you have to tell them of Christ. It's about prayer. The fight for souls is a spiritual battle.

> For we are not fighting against people made of flesh and blood, but against the evil rulers and authorities of the unseen world, against those mighty powers of darkness who rule this world, against the wicked spirits in the heavenly realms. (EPHESIANS 6:12 NLT)

If you are going to be a part of that battle, you must use the weapon of prayer. Spend time on your knees praying for the souls of your teammates. Remember, on a spiritual battleground, prayer is where the victory will be won.

Here are a few practical things that will help you as you pray for your teammates:

Pray specifically. Pray for them by name. Pray they will be convicted of sin and see the truth of the gospel. Pray God's Spirit will help them to see themselves as God does. Pray God will give you opportunities to talk with them about spiritual things. Pray about specific issues in their lives.

Pray persistently. No matter how long it takes, keep praying for them. Mark certain days on your calendar and set aside time to pray for them. Keep a prayer list to remind you to pray on a regular basis for them.

Pray expectantly. The Bible says in Matthew 21:22, "And all things you ask in prayer, believing, you will receive." Expect God to answer your prayer. Remember, it is His desire to see people come to know Him.

> The Lord is not slow about His promise, as some count slowness, but is patient toward you, not wishing for any to perish but for all to come to repentance. (2 PETER 3:9)

102

BE SURE HE WILL USE YOU

God has given you as an athlete an extraordinary opportunity to be used by Him in the lives of your teammates. The very reason you have been blessed with athletic ability may be for the purpose of impacting the life of a teammate. Don't underestimate the fact that God can and will use you to reach your teammates and make a difference for His glory.

The noted evangelist Billy Sunday was won to Christ through the influence of a batboy's sister, while he was playing professional baseball. Keep in mind that although your teammates may be the most difficult to reach, because you are close to them, you have great opportunities to impact their lives for Jesus Christ. I have known of hundreds of athletes who became Christians through the influence of a teammate. God will use you! Take advantage of every opportunity He provides! Use every resource at your disposal to be a witness for Him! He will do the rest!

To Think About

1. List the names of your teammates who are probably not Christians.

2. Is there any area in your life that needs to change for you to have an effective witness to them?

3. Match one of the following possible witnessing approaches to each non-Christian on your team.

   • Share your testimony

   • Give them a tract

   • Invite them to church

   • Invite them to a Christian concert

   • Give them a Christian book

   • Pray for them

ACCEPTING YOUR PLATFORM

[YOU] WILL TELL PEOPLE
ABOUT ME EVERY-
WHERE—IN JERUSALEM,
THROUGHOUT JUDEA,
IN SAMARIA, AND TO
THE ENDS OF THE EARTH.
(ACTS 1:8 NLT)

Influence. The dictionary defines it as "the power to affect others." For the athlete, that power is tremendous. In 1996 it was estimated to have been worth more than $13 billion in sporting goods endorsements. But the influence of the athlete is much bigger than its worth in selling shoes. It can be seen in the spin move of a youngster trying to be like his favorite NBA player—and likewise in the example of a junior high football player to an onlooking peer. The reach of the athlete's influence is not bound by sex, age, or ability. It simply is a part of being an athlete in today's society.

Jesus said the influence of every Christian is important and is designed for a specific purpose.

> You are the light of the world. A city set on a hill cannot be hidden; nor does anyone light a lamp and put it under a basket, but on the lampstand, and it gives light to all who are in the house. Let your light shine before men in such a way that they may see your good works, and glorify your Father who is in heaven. (MATTHEW 5:14–16)

YOU ARE AN INFLUENCE

Two important truths about influence are seen in that passage. *The first and most basic is that you* are *an influence.* "You are the light of the world. A city set on a hill cannot be hidden." The Bible says your life is like a brightly lit city that sits high on a hill and can be seen from far away. Light is a powerful influence.

Have you ever been in a dark place? I mean really dark—so dark that your eyes never got used to it? When you light a match, what does that do to the darkness? Is there anyplace so dark that you can't see light when it is introduced? The truth is, light can always be seen in the darkness. Anytime light and darkness meet, light always comes out the winner.

As a representative of Jesus Christ, you are light. You have influence. Being an athlete sets your life on a hill, and folks are watching you. You may never even be aware of the impact you have.

Bobby Jones, former NBA great, tells of speaking at a program a few years ago. After the event was over, all-pro defensive end Reggie White came over for a word with him. He said, "Bobby, I want to thank you for the influence you have had on my life." Bobby said, "What do you mean?" Reggie explained, "When I was in junior high school, I was at an FCA camp where you spoke. My favorite team was the 76ers, and you took some extra time with me at camp. That had a big influence on me. Thanks."

You may never know of the influence you have and the lives you may be touching. Professional basketball player A. C. Green shares his perspective on the influence of an athlete in his book *Victory:*

> *Everyone has influence, and everyone is responsible for how he uses it. Those of us who have more influence just have more responsibility. God has given me an honor to play professional basketball, but with that honor comes a duty to myself, to God and to others.*[1]

Record-setting NFL receiver Chris Carter explains his view on using his influence this way:

I have a purpose in life. And it is to use the platform I have been given so that God's name might be glorified. God calls me to be truthful, to be frank and to step out in faith. I am responsible to use my influence and my resources for His glory.[2]

There is no question that an athlete in today's society has an immense amount of influence. That influence likewise carries an immense amount of responsibility for the athlete who is a Christian—a responsibility to use it for the Lord.

USE YOUR INFLUENCE

The second truth concerning influence seen in this passage is that God wants to use your influence for His work. "Let your light shine before men in such a way that they may see your good works, and glorify your Father who is in heaven." It is God who has blessed you with the talents and abilities you possess. He gave you those abilities for a specific purpose—to be used for His glory. Let Him accomplish His purpose in your life. Live as you ought and take advantage of opportunities to speak of your faith.

One high school athlete had it in perspective when he said, "The day I stop using sports to witness for Jesus Christ is the day I should quit!" God has given you as a Christian athlete a unique and unprecedented platform for impacting lives for Jesus Christ. Go for it!

Athletes have all kinds of opportunities. For those who find themselves in the limelight, the media interview presents an excellent platform. In the past, reporters and broadcasters would run when a Christian athlete mentioned anything about God. Now, coaches and athletes alike are even interviewed about their faith and spiritual orientation. Even the high school athlete has a voice in the media with the detailed sports coverage of most local stations.

Joe DeLoach won the gold medal in the 200-meter run in Seoul. He beat Carl Lewis in the finals and set the world record. I spoke with Joe, an outstanding Christian, and asked him about the importance of communicating his faith. He responded:

Anytime you get something good you want to tell somebody about it. When I won the Olympic gold, I ran up a big telephone bill calling from Seoul,

Korea: "Did you see it? Did you see it? I actually did it!" So when we come into a relationship with God, it's the same way. Once we are saved, God wants us to be in this crooked and evil and perverted generation of darkness like neon signs saying, "Try Jesus. Try Jesus!" That's what God really wants for us. And when we do that, not only are we blessed but the world gets to share our blessing. It's like when I stood on the Olympic awards platform. All of the people that knew me, their hearts fluttered because they knew Joe DeLoach. They shared in my glory and my victory. And others can do that as well when we become a witness for the Lord.

LOOK FOR THE OBVIOUS OPPORTUNITIES

What are some other ways you can let your light shine? First, look for the obvious opportunities right in front of you. Those opportunities may be speaking engagements, taking a stand as a leader on your team, or giving credit to the Lord in an interview. God will put you in situations where you can shine and at the same time give you boldness to speak out. Jim Ryun tells of his experiences in becoming a witness for the Lord:

As a normal outgrowth of the deeper dimensions of our Christian experience came the desire to share the Lord's love with those we met. The Lord gradually replaced my previous reticence with a great love for people and enthusiasm to share with them and get to know them. Simply put, I just began to enjoy people. Where once I had been extremely self-centered, I could look at other people and share their joys, their sorrows—pray with them and for them, help them where I could. I could not keep inside my desire for them to experience the quality of life I myself had discovered with the Lord. So it became the most natural thing of all to tell people I met about what he had done for us. I discovered myself unbound to speak with and relate to people on a new level. It became a great joy and privilege when I was asked to speak rather than the nightmare any public exposure had been earlier in my life. My former shyness fell away and was replaced by a great love for people.[3]

DO THE SMALL THINGS

There are many small things you can do to witness to others, taking advantage of unique opportunities you may have because you are an athlete. It may be putting a verse of Scripture on an autograph, praying before or after a game, or quoting a Bible verse during an interview.

One Division 1 cross-country athlete tapes Scripture verses on the back of his shoes when he races. He says it not only is a witness to others, but it also inspires him to run well enough to stay in front of other runners so they can see the backs of his shoes.

Another way you can be a witness is to wear a T-shirt with a verse or statement about the Lord printed on it. Witnessing can also be as simple as carrying your Bible. The important thing is to take advantage of every opportunity God puts in front of you.

> And if you are asked about your Christian hope, always be ready to explain it. But you must do this in a gentle and respectful way. Keep your conscience clear. Then if people speak evil against you, they will be ashamed when they see what a good life you live because you belong to Christ. (1 PETER 3:15–16 NLT)

BE AN EXAMPLE

Still another way to let your light shine is to be an example to those who watch you and look up to you. Your behavior and actions are always in the spotlight. That is not always an easy responsibility to bear, but it is nevertheless still a responsibility you must face.

Orel Hershiser tells of the unique challenges of being a witness and a high-profile athlete:

> *I'm not one to wear my faith on my sleeve. Christians can do a disservice to unbelievers by being obnoxious or judgmental. I'm a chapel leader and have been since my second year in the minors. People know where I am coming from without having to harp on it all the time. I know that the message of Christ offends because it calls sin sin and says we are all sinners. There's no way to soften that truth. It's jarring and can alienate people until they begin to realize that it's true. My pushing it down everyone's throat will not make it any easier for them to investigate what it's all about.*
>
> *I just tell people about God naturally, when opportunities arise or when I'm asked. It's amazing how many people notice when you tend to be straight. If you are not a carouser, not a womanizer, not foul-mouthed, not a gossip, it gets around.*[4]

It is important to remember that you represent Jesus Christ at all times. People are watching you. It's like when you put on your team's uniform. The colors and emblems are associated with your school or team. When you wear that uniform, you represent your team. In the same way, when you are a Christian, you are Christ's representative.

We are ambassadors for Christ, as though God were making an appeal through us; we beg you on behalf of Christ, be reconciled to God. (2 CORINTHIANS 5:20)

Chad Hennings has experienced this as a member of one of the best-known athletic teams in America. He writes:

As a member of the Cowboys, I'm in the public eye. I see that as a big responsibility and as an opportunity to further the kingdom of God. For that reason, I realize how important it is that I conduct myself not merely as an ambassador for the Dallas Cowboys, but as an ambassador for the Lord Jesus Christ. Whether I'm out to dinner with friends or going to the gas station to fill the truck with gas, people are watching me, curious to see how I conduct myself. They want to know, Is this guy a fence-straddler or a hypocrite—or does he really live what he says he believes?

It's a responsibility I take very seriously, and that is why I always try to keep in mind who I'm representing.[5]

The first chapel service I ever held for a major league team was for the Minnesota Twins. Everyone on the team came to the service. In all the years that have passed since, that is the only time I have ever witnessed an entire team coming to chapel. I thought they came because they heard that I was going to be the speaker. The real reason they came was that there was a handful of Christians on the team that were for real. Something about their lives had earned the respect of their teammates. And so they came to chapel.

One of these guys later became one of my closest friends. His name was Danny Thompson. Danny was from a small town in Oklahoma with a population less than a hundred, and that was counting the chickens and the dogs. He had four in his graduating class —all guys. Needless to say, the senior prom wasn't much fun.

110

But Danny was quite a ballplayer, and he went on to be all-American at Oklahoma State. Drafted by the Minnesota Twins, he became their starting shortstop in the early '70s and thus fulfilled a dream he'd had since boyhood. The only problem was that when he finally saw his picture on a bubblegum card, it didn't do for him what he thought it would. There was still something missing.

Through the influence of some Christian athletes on the team, Danny discovered that what was missing from his life was a personal relationship with Jesus Christ. So he trusted in Him to be his Lord and Savior. Shortly after that time, during a routine physical, he discovered that he had leukemia. This was devastating news, but Danny was determined not only to continue to succeed as an athlete but to make his life count for Jesus Christ. He would take advantage of any opportunity he had to share his dynamic testimony.

Midway through the season in 1976, Danny was traded to the Texas Rangers. I had just done chapel for them, and only four guys had shown up. (They probably did hear I was coming.) In the course of the off-season, three of the four were traded, and the other retired. So there was not a lot of Christian witness on the team when Danny arrived. In a matter of a few weeks, however, five new Christians were on the team. I did chapel again not long after that, and more than twenty guys were there. It was all because of the influence of one man.

Let me tell you what that says to me. If God, through one guy, can do that with a bunch of hotdog, superstar, professional athletes, there is no limit to what He can do through you, whoever you are. In Acts 17, Paul and Silas went into a city and were accused of turning the world upside down. That's what God wants to do through you in your school, on your team, in your city, with your platform.

On December 13, 1976, more than five hundred people crowded into a little high school auditorium in Burlington, Oklahoma, for Danny Thompson's funeral service. As I stood to speak that day, I was struck by the awesome influence that Danny's platform had given him. Ballplayers and others from all over the country were there, people whose lives would never be the same because one player realized he had an influence and let God use him.

Use your influence to make a difference for the Lord. It may be the very reason that God has blessed you with athletic ability. Make it count for eternity.

To Think About

1. When the Bible says, "You are the light of the world," what does that mean to you as an athlete?

2. What are some practical things you can do as an athlete to let people know you are a Christian?

3. Why is your behavior on the field of competition important to your witness?

4. What areas need to change for you to be an effective witness to those who see you compete?

FINISHING THE RACE

**I HAVE FOUGHT
THE GOOD FIGHT,
I HAVE FINISHED THE
COURSE, I HAVE
KEPT THE FAITH.**
(2 TIMOTHY 4:7)

T here is a great scene from the movie *Cool Runnings,* based on a true incident from the 1988 Winter Olympics. The inexperienced bobsled team from Jamaica, in their first trip to the Olympics, borrows a sled and makes their first ever run when they arrive for the practice rounds. Surprisingly, going into the last round of competition, they find themselves in possible contention for a medal. However, the sled malfunctions on their last run and sends them out of control down the hill, crashing short of the finish line. Onlookers rush to help them and discover that, miraculously, no one is seriously injured.

Their dream of a medal ended, they pick up the damaged sled, put it on their shoulders, and carry it to the finish line, to the rousing applause of the crowd. They didn't win the race, but they finished it. They didn't finish on time, but they finished well.

We have discussed a number of things that, hopefully, have helped you to better understand what God expects from a Christian athlete. We have dealt with the importance of focusing on and pleasing one fan in the stands, Jesus Christ. We have examined the ultimate goal of becoming like Him. We have also looked at the obstacles and hindrances to accomplishing God's plan as well as the necessity of giving your all to please Him. We have learned how to face pressure and deal with setbacks and difficulties. And finally, we have seen how God wants to use the physical gifts He has blessed you with to influence both your teammates and others who see you.

For the Christian athlete, finishing the race well is putting all those things into practice. It's being everything God wants you to be and allowing Him to do everything He wants to do through you. It is measured by a couple of important standards.

Finishing well is measured, first, not by awards or recognition but by your personal relationship with God. Don't lose that focus. Nothing is more important than your relationship with Him.

Golfer Paul Azinger has come to understand this important key. He writes:

> I don't know how successful you are. I don't know how big your house is, how much money you have, or how nice your car is, or how nice your boat is. But I'm telling you, we came into this world with nothing, and we are leaving with nothing. And everything we get along the way is a blessing from God. If you are finding your contentment and happiness in your accomplishments, or from the amount of money and possessions you own, I am here to tell you, it doesn't last.
>
> Even though it is great to be called a PGA Tour player, and it's probably even greater to be called a PGA champion, no greater gift is mine than to be called a child of God, because I place my trust in Jesus Christ.[1]

The second key to finishing the race well for the Christian athlete is keeping your focus on pleasing the Lord.

Michelle Akers, captain of the World Cup Champion U.S. women's soccer team, has her priorities straight when she says:

> Don't get caught up in what your friends think is important or winning the trophy at all costs. Yes, try hard. Train hard. Make sacrifices to be a good soccer player and a good athlete. But when it all comes down to the final day and you look in the mirror and you have to face yourself—I'd rather see myself as a godly person than as a world championship soccer player.[2]

I have already told you about my eventful first season as a high school baseball coach. The second year for our team, we picked up a few more athletes and finished with a pretty good record. It was good enough to qualify us for the Tri-State Christian High School Championships. This was a tournament involving all the best teams from Oklahoma, Missouri, and Kansas.

We played well and wound up in the championship game despite losing our best pitcher to an injury in the semifinals. The game matched us against the number one seed, a team with a very impressive record and a lot of talent. Our guys fought hard and tied the game in the bottom of the eighth, 4–4. Our defense held them in the top of the ninth, and we came to bat in the bottom half of the inning with a chance to win the game and the championship.

Our leadoff hitter, Frank, reached first, beating the throw for an infield single. He stole second when the next batter struck out and went to third on a sacrifice fly. Here we are, two outs, bottom of the ninth, score tied, in the championship game. Everyone in the stands is yelling instructions to Frank. The assistant coach is trying to tell him what to do from the first-base box. The players on the other team are screaming other things at him. I leaned over to him (I was coaching third) and said, "Frank, no matter what happens, listen to me. Don't pay attention to anyone else."

He nodded and took his lead. The next pitch was in the dirt and hit the catcher in the foot, rolling a little past him. The batter immediately jumped up and waved Frank back to third. From the corner of my eye, I could see the fans behind the backstop doing the same, while they screamed similar instructions. At the same time, as if it were all happening in slow motion, I simply said, "Frank, go!" And with every fiber in his body he sprinted toward home and slid in just under the tag. We won the game and the championship!

Over the years I have reflected a great deal on that moment— the excitement, the noise, the fun of it all—just winning the championship. Yet, far more than the victory, I am most inspired by Frank's wholehearted focus on his coach's voice. In spite of all the distractions, the pressure, and all the fans in the stands, he zeroed in on one voice and gave his complete all to follow those instructions. That is a picture of real success for the Christian athlete.

Wherever athletics has taken you or may take you, when it's all said and done, it boils down to the voice you listened to. Were you focused on Him? Was *He* pleased with your performance?

When all the awards are given out and the jerseys are put away, there is only one phrase of approval that is eternal. And it comes from God the Father: "Well done, good and faithful servant!" (Matthew 25:21 NIV).

That is the measure of finishing well. That is the ultimate measure of real success.

TO MOMS AND DADS

There is an old sign leaning against one of the weight machines at the health club where I used to work out. Someone salvaged it when they tore down the old high school football stadium years ago. The words on the sign represent a philosophy about athletics that, sadly, was also torn down a long time ago. The sign reads:

> With the profound thought that clean sportsmanship instills in our youth the finest and truest principles of life, this stadium is dedicated to the Wichita Falls Independent School District by the Kiwanis Club of Wichita Falls, Texas.
>
> October 9, 1931

What has happened to the idea that sports is about teaching the finest and truest principles of life? That used to be the point of athletics. Sports today has gone in the completely opposite direction. Athletic competition now demonstrates and teaches the ugliest and worst principles of life. The standards of modern athletics seem to be:

1. Win at all cost.
2. If someone hits you, hit him back.
3. It is what the sport does for you, not what you do for the sport.
4. If you do poorly, it is someone else's fault, such as the coach or referee.
5. Gripe about everything.
6. He who talks the best trash looks the best.
7. You are worthless if you do not win.

Somewhere we drifted far away from the idea of using athletics to prepare our children for true success in life. And I am afraid that much of the responsibility for this falls on the shoulders of parents. In spite of all of the talk about pro athletes being role models and the powerful influence of the media in the lives of kids, experts still tell us that parents have more influence on their children's attitudes and actions than anyone else.

How can you as a parent help your child to experience real success in athletics? Obviously, the principles of success we have discussed in this book are essentials that all parents need to help their children learn and apply. However, let us examine here several specific things that every parent can do to help his child experience real success in athletics and in life.

HELP YOUR CHILDREN UNDERSTAND THE DEFINITION OF REAL SUCCESS

First, help your children understand that awards, recognition, and accomplishments are not the ultimate measure of success. Let's briefly review from chapter 2 the most common misunderstandings about success as an athlete. Real success is not:

1. Reaching the top of your profession
2. Staying at the top of your profession
3. Becoming well-known
4. Obtaining material wealth

Mom and Dad, let me add the following about your athlete children. Real success is not:

5. Receiving all-district honors
6. Making the varsity team
7. Starting on the team
8. Being the *best* player on the team
9. Accomplishing *your* plan for their lives

True success can only be measured by being the best they can be. It is the most that can be realistically expected of them.

Several years ago I was speaking at a basketball camp where the camp leaders gave every kid an award sometime during the week. The coaches watched for a moment when each kid was at his best and would make up a crazy award for it. They gave out awards such as the "He Hustled Like a Big Dog" award and the "If Only Your Mama Could Have Seen That Rebound" award. What a great concept! It helped every kid understand that the measurement of real success is being the best they can be.

Hall of Fame linebacker Mike Singletary and his wife emphasize this with their children. He writes:

> As I tell our children, do your best, but don't be overly concerned with winning. And don't get wrapped up in thinking about yourself, or how many awards you'll win, or how much applause or recognition you will receive. Keep your ego in check.
>
> Just put your nose to the grindstone and go to work. Decide what it takes to be the best you can possibly be, then strive with all your heart and might to accomplish that one thing.
>
> I don't care whether we're talking about building a better mousetrap or making the highest score on the college boards. Just give it your all.[1]

Find that moment when your child is giving his all and encourage him for it. It may be his effort in practice, it might come in a game, or it may just be the way he encourages his teammates from the bench. If you as a parent reinforce that behavior, your children will begin to see it as a priority.

BE AN EXAMPLE OF THE KIND OF BEHAVIOR
YOU WANT THEM TO DEMONSTRATE

Therefore be imitators of God, as beloved children. (EPHESIANS 5:1)

Recently, I read about a mother who got so upset during her eleven-year-old son's soccer game that she went down on the field and punched the referee. She was banned from attending games for three years, as well as given a fine and a six-months' probation. That means her son could be fifteen before she watches him play another game.

In my years as a coach and as a parent of two athletes, the worst behavior I have ever witnessed has not come from the players but, instead, from their parents. I have watched dads angrily run out on the field and interrupt a game. I have seen moms fighting in the stands during a game. And, sadly, I have watched parents berate their own children in front of a packed arena because of a mistake or a poor performance. Your children will not demonstrate a proper perspective of real success unless you first understand it and then demonstrate it for them.

It is important to remember that athletics resembles life in many ways. When your child learns the right way to respond to losing a game, it will help him know how to deal with losing a job someday. When children can overcome bad calls from the referee, they can overcome difficulties they will face later in their lives. Show them how to do it. Model proper behavior for your children. Be an example to them.

EMPHASIZE BEING *THEIR* BEST
RATHER THAN BEING *THE* BEST

There is a lot of emphasis in athletics on being the best. The problem with that emphasis is that there is only room for one person to be the best. Every team but one ends the season with a loss. Where does that leave the others? Are they losers? Of course not. It is not good to emphasize being the best. The correct focus is to help your children be *their* best. That, after all, is true success. What can you do to help your child be his best?

The best thing you can do is to keep the focus away from winning, losing, scores, or statistics. Instead, help your children to emphasize being the very best they can be. Take, for example, two high school athletes, Stephen and Doug. Stephen's parents measure their son's success by whether or not he is the team's leading scorer in the game. The problem with this is that it puts enormous pressure on Stephen; if he doesn't meet their expectations, he thinks he is a loser. Ultimately that pressure hinders his performance in the game because he is always thinking about scoring. I have watched him cry in the locker room after a *victory,* because he was not the leading scorer.

On the other hand, Doug's parents have reinforced the standard of simply being the best he can be. When Doug plays in a game, he knows that all he has to focus on is doing his best. No matter the outcome of the game, he is a winner. He is not burdened down by unnecessary pressure. He can go out, play hard, and enjoy the experience.

Stephen's parents provide prime examples of the problems that arise when parents are not focused on the proper motivation. As a parent, you need to help alleviate pressures on your children any way you can, not produce them. Ask them after every game, "Were you the best you could be?" Encourage them when they work hard. If you value wholehearted performance, they will, too.

KEEP THE PROPER PERSPECTIVE
ON YOUR CHILD'S ABILITIES AND FUTURE

Recently, I overheard a conversation between a high school football coach and the mother of one of his players. The coach was trying to explain that the woman's son was on the line between the junior varsity and varsity and that he was having a hard time trying to decide where to put the boy.

The parent's immediate response was, "If you put him on JV, we'll just quit! He's the best guy you have out there." Although her son was a very good athlete, the parent had an unrealistic estimation of her son's abilities. In reality, he was small and inexperienced.

One of the most difficult things for a parent to do is to have an accurate perception of his child's abilities. Every parent wants to believe his child is the best in everything he does. Realistically, that is rarely the case. Don't get me wrong. It is important for your children to know you believe in them, but an unfair assessment of their abilities can set them up for failure. I have seen kids quit the team because their parents were convinced that the coach was an idiot for not recognizing the future Hall-of-Fame talent in their child. Sure, sometimes coaches miss it, but you are far better off as a parent by helping your children to trust the coach and continue to give their best.

When my son was in the seventh grade, he didn't play as much as I thought he should. However, instead of griping and grumbling and ruining his attitude, the two of us focused on how he could encourage and cheer his teammates when he was on the bench. It helped him learn to be a part of the team. In the years to follow, when he did start to play a great deal, he was a much better team leader because of his ability to encourage his teammates.

Ambrose Robinson, father of NBA superstar David Robinson, offers this insight from his experience:

> Sports was just an outlet, something to do for rest and relaxation. We never looked at it as a possible livelihood. I think that is a mistake some parents make these days. They're playing baseball and football in the backyard, hoping their children will become pro sports heroes when they grow up. That's not the way to do it, in my opinion. If it happens, all's well and good. But I don't think you can groom a pro athlete. You talk to numerous pro athletes, and they'll tell you they had no idea when they were youngsters that they'd be playing pro sports. They might have emulated certain heroes, but I don't think parents should push it because such a small percentage who try to go pro make it.[2]

Help your child learn character as he participates in athletics. If your child excels and becomes a superstar, he will have what it takes on the inside, if you have laid the proper foundation. To be realistic, the odds are against your child's making it to the big time. Out of 1,223 high school seniors playing football, only 44 will still be playing when they are seniors in college. Out of those 44, only 1 will make the roster of an NFL team. Only 1 out of 963,000 high school seniors playing basketball will make an NBA team. What does all this say? It is highly unlikely that your child will become a professional athlete. So relax and enjoy the time he does spend in sports. Don't take it so seriously.

SHOW THEM THAT THEIR WORTH
DOES NOT HINGE ON THEIR PERFORMANCE

A friend of mine played football for one of the top college programs in the nation. He was an exceptional athlete and ultimately finished his career in the NFL with a Super Bowl championship. Sadly, his greatest obstacle was his father. Once, after rushing for more than 300 yards and leading his team to victory in a key college contest, his dad came down to the locker room and berated him for losing a couple of fumbles in the game. There was not a word about the 300 yards gained or the victory, only harsh words about his son's shortcomings.

The young man was devastated. These incidents became so much of a problem that finally the coach banned the dad from the locker room. Whatever his father's intentions were, the message he was communicating to his boy was "No matter how you play, you always will fall short in my eyes." What his son needed more than anything else from his dad was to know that, however he played, he was loved.

Your child must know that, if he scores twenty points or turns over the ball more than twenty times, your love for him does not change. Don't just assume he knows that. Look him in the eyes and say, "If you get all A's or flunk out of school, I will still love you with all of my heart. If you lead your team to the state championship or decide to never play again, I will love you with all the love I have. There is nothing you can do that will change how much I love you!"

Joe White counsels countless teens and parents each year. He is the president of Kanakuk-Kanakomo Kamps, Inc., near Branson, Missouri. He writes in his book *What Kids Wish Parents Knew About Parenting*:

I can't stress enough how much kids today need to hear and feel that un-

conditional love from their parents, over and over and over again. It's the pivotal need in their lives, and when it's received, it forms the apex of their hearts. It gives them the necessary strength and courage to face every pressure, day after day, for the rest of their lives.[3]

White goes on to tell of his own story as an athlete and his relationship with his father:

I'll never forget his love, acceptance, and words of wisdom the day I came home sobbing after finding out my best buddy had gotten a starting position on the football team and I was to sit on the bench. Later, as a tiny noseguard at Southern Methodist University, I got clobbered Saturday after heartbreaking Saturday. Daddy was always there. I grew to depend on seeing his kind and encouraging face outside the locker room after a game. He didn't care about the score. He cared about me.[4]

Does your son or daughter feel that way about you after a game? Do your son and daughter know for sure that you don't care about the score, you care about them? If your child had a poor performance, believe me, someone has already pointed it out to him, and it was probably some bozo in the stands. Don't take sides with the bozo. Take sides with your child. Love him, hug him, and encourage him the same after every game regardless of the outcome.

SHOW THEM LOVE BY BEING THERE FOR THEM

I don't believe anyone in the history of the world has ever come to the end of his life and said, "If only I had spent more time at work," or, "Why didn't I watch more television?" Sadly, I have heard many say, "If only I had spent more time with my family." Family experts agree that when it comes to your children, love is spelled T-I-M-E.

I believe that, as the parent of athletes, there is nothing more important you can do than to be there for them. This means you need to do whatever you have to do to be at your children's games. It is important to them. They need to hear you cheering for them. They need to see that what they do is important to you.

Now there are some legitimate circumstances that keep parents from attending their children's activities. The single parent faces time demands that are very difficult to balance. It is also tough trying to manage the schedule in a family with several children participating in a variety of activities. But, whatever your demands, invest every possible minute in the lives of your children.

There was a young man who played basketball with my son one year in high school. He probably played a total of five or six minutes the whole thirty-game season. What impressed me was that his parents came to every game, home or away. That's truly impressive. There is a kid who knows that his parents love and support him, no matter what.

I made a decision when my son went to high school that I would not miss any of his games. That meant certain sacrifices had to be made. I had to cancel several speaking engagements. I had to use some vacation days that could have gone for something else. I also had to give up a good night's rest before a big workday in order to make a long drive—but *it was worth it!* Your child's athletic career is a relatively short period of time in your life. Don't look back with regret someday, knowing you could have done things differently. Do whatever it takes to let your children see you in the stands. It is important to them.

SHOW THEM LOVE BY ENCOURAGING THEM

I will never forget my sixth grade teacher, Mr. Rupp. My favorite part of school in the sixth grade was music. I loved music. I loved to sing. Every week he would pick a couple of students to come up to the front of the room, and they would get to sing. In the course of the entire school year, he never once picked me to sing in front of the class.

One day he called me to his desk and explained why I would never get a turn. He told me it was because I was a loser and I would never amount to anything. Now maybe he was trying to use some kind of reverse psychology on me in order to motivate me to be a better person. I really don't give him that much credit, but it doesn't matter because the approach was wrong no matter how you look at it. Those words were painful and devastating.

Contrast Mr. Rupp with my seventh grade music teacher, Mrs. White. The first week of school, she told me I had a great voice and

THE RIGHT WAY TO WIN

asked me to be in a special men's ensemble. She told me she wanted me to sit on the front row in choir class so that my voice would stand out. I spent two years in her choirs and singing groups, had a lead in the eighth grade musical, and went on to be very involved in music in high school and college.

I have since sung for movie stars, politicians, countless professional athletes, company presidents, multimillionaires, college students, farmers, and everyday people from one end of the country to another. I have published songs, recorded albums, and have had my songs recorded by other artists. I once even sang the national anthem for the Monday Night Game of the Week on national television. All I have to say about it all is, "Mr. Rupp, wherever you are, *you missed it! Mrs. White, wherever you are, thanks for the encouragement!*"

The Bible says, "Therefore encourage one another and build up one another, just as you also are doing" (1 Thessalonians 5:11). Your children need to hear words of encouragement from you. If they don't play, tell them you are proud of their patience and hard work. If they go 0 for 6 at the plate or have a few turnovers in a game, remind them it is just a game. Encourage them and build them up.

I talked with a young man who, despite his great talent, dropped out of a major college sports program because he didn't have the heart for it anymore. His greatest frustration was going home after a game, where all he ever heard from his dad was how he could have done better. He told me, "Everybody in the world can tell you that you are good, but if you don't hear it from your parents, it doesn't matter."

Mom and Dad, you have the power to build up your children and help them be the best they can be or tear them down with your words or lack of them.

REMEMBER THE REAL PRIORITY

Teach your children to choose the right path, and when they are older, they will remain upon it. (PROVERBS 22:6 NLT)

When in junior high school, Jimmy was a leader in his youth group at church. He spent those two years being discipled by his youth minister and even considered that God might be calling him into the ministry.

His freshman year in high school, Jimmy began to be recognized as a standout soccer player. After some encouragement from the coach, his parents signed him up for an out-of-town league that played on weekends. Because of his soccer commitments, it was difficult for him (and his parents) to be very involved in church. Over a period of time, the boy's emphasis gradually shifted away from his relationship to God. A knee injury ultimately ended his athletic career early in college.

Now that soccer is over for him, Jimmy spends his Sunday mornings sleeping in and recovering from his late-night drinking and partying. The problem here is that Jimmy's parents lost sight of the real priority. What they thought was important was short-lived. What they thought was harmless had a long-lasting and perhaps permanent negative impact on Jimmy's life.

Regrettably, this is a story that is repeated in the lives of many young Christian athletes every weekend. Youth ministers will tell you that the number one competition they have on Sundays is youth athletics. And it is not just a few Sundays; it is fifty-two weeks out of the year.

If you build a foundation of baseball or soccer in the lives of your children, you have built a foundation that is very temporary. If their priority is sports, what happens to them when their athletic career is over? Don't forget the real priority. If it comes down to missing two summer league games or missing youth camp at church, pick the one that will have the most lasting impact. What does it profit a young man or woman if he wins the city championship and loses his soul?

Jesus said, "[God] will give you all you need from day to day if you live for him and make the Kingdom of God your primary concern" (Matthew 6:33 NLT). Keep the Lord first in your life and in the lives of your children. Enjoy their participation in athletics and use those experiences as opportunities to teach them, to nurture them, and to love them. That is the right way to win.

To Think About

1. What positive characteristics can be developed in the life of your child through participation in athletics?

2. What practical things can you can do to encourage your children to be their best rather than being the best?

3. What do you want your child to get out of his or her athletic experience?

4. If you were to ask your children what they thought were your priorities for them in athletics, what would they say?

5. What are some ways you can express unconditional love to your children?

NOTES

CHAPTER 1

1. Shirl J. Hoffman, *Sport and Religion* (Champaign, Ill.: Human Kinetics Publishing, 1992), 178.
2. Bernard Holyfield and Evander Holyfield, *Holyfield the Humble Warrior* (Nashville: Nelson, 1996), 98–101.
3. David Fisher and Ron Luciano, *Strike Two* (New York: Bantam, 1985), 113.
4. David Fisher and Ron Luciano, *The Fall of the Roman Umpire* (New York: Bantam, 1986), 259.

CHAPTER 2

1. Pat Williams, *Go for the Magic* (Nashville: Nelson, 1995), 221.
2. Chad Hennings, *It Takes Commitment* (Sisters, Ore.: Multnomah Press, 1996), 155.
3. Christin Ditchfield, "Holding Serve," *Sports Spectrum* (August 1996): 8.

CHAPTER 3

1. Shane Murphy, *The Achievement Zone* (New York: Berkley Books, 1996), 142.
2. Wes Neal, *The Handbook on Athletic Perfection* (Prescott, Ariz.: Institute for Athletic Perfection, 1975), 39.
3. Darrell Porter, *Snap Me Perfect! The Darrell Porter Story* (Nashville: Nelson, 1984), 252.
4. A. C. Green, *Victory* (Orlando, Fla.: Creation House, 1994), 42–43.

CHAPTER 4

1. Bill Bates, *Shoot for the Stars* (Dallas: Word, 1994), 38.
2. John Dodderidge, "Humility on the Diamond," *Sharing the Victory* (April 1996): 6.
3. Rob Bentz, "Mister Big," *Sports Spectrum* (August 1996): 19.
4. Christin Ditchfield, "Holding Serve," *Sports Spectrum* (August 1996): 6.
5. A.C. Green, *Victory* (Orlando, Fla.: Creation House, 1994), 23.

CHAPTER 5

1. Chad Hennings, *It Takes Commitment* (Sisters, Ore.: Multnomah Press, 1996), 181.
2. Reggie White, *In the Trenches* (Nashville: Nelson, 1996), 245.
3. Steve Jamison and John Wooden, *Wooden* (Chicago: Contemporary Books, 1997), 176.
4. Darrel Campbell and Pete Maravich, *Heir to a Dream* (Nashville: Nelson, 1987), 75.
5. Catherine Swift, *Eric Liddell* (Minneapolis: Bethany House, 1990), 84–85.
6. Orel Hershiser, *Out of the Blue* (Brentwood, Tenn.: Wolgemuth & Hyatt, 1989), 24.
7. Source unknown.

CHAPTER 6

1. Reggie White, *In the Trenches* (Nashville: Nelson, 1996), 248.

CHAPTER 7

1. Steve Jamison and John Wooden, *Wooden* (Chicago: Contemporary Books, 1997), 58.
2. Quoted by Mark Todd, "The Goal and Focus of a Champion," *Sharing the Victory* (April, 1996): 13.

CHAPTER 8

1. Mickey Mantle, "Time in a Bottle," *Sports Illustrated* (April 18, 1994): 74.
2. Jim Ryun, *In Quest of Gold* (Lawrence, Kans.: Ryun and Sons Publishing, 1995), 188.
3. Del Reddy and Trent Thomson, "A Broadcasting Legend," *Sharing the Victory* (March 1993): 18.
4. Paul Azinger, *Zinger* (Grand Rapids: Zondervan, 1995), 206.

CHAPTER 10

1. A. C. Green, *Victory* (Orlando, Fla.: Creation House, 1994), 229.
2. Quoted by David Moriah, "Great Catch," *Sports Spectrum* (October 1995): 18.
3. Jim Ryun, *In Quest of Gold* (Lawrence, Kan.: Ryun and Sons Publishing, 1995), 188.
4. Orel Herschiser, *Out of the Blue* (Brentwood, Tenn.: Wolgemuth & Hyatt, 1989), 85.
5. Chad Hennings, *It Takes Commitment* (Sisters, Ore.: Multnomah Press, 1996), 149.

CHAPTER 11

1. Paul Azinger, *Zinger* (New York: Harper Paperbacks, 1995), 250–51.
2. Judy Douglass and Steve Jessup, "The Golden Boot," *Sports Spectrum* (June 1996): 29.

TO MOMS AND DADS

1. Mike Singletary with Russ Pate, *Daddy's Home at Last* (Grand Rapids: Zondervan, 1998), 177.
2. Ambrose Robinson and Freda Robinson with Steve Hubbard, *How to Raise an MVP* (Grand Rapids: Zondervan, 1996), 126.

3. Joe White, *What Kids Wish Parents Knew About Parenting* (West Monroe, La.: Howard Publishing, 1998), 69–70.

4. Ibid.

Moody Press, a ministry of Moody Bible Institute, is designed for education, evangelization, and edification. If we may assist you in knowing more about Christ and the Christian life, please write us without obligation: Moody Press, c/o MLM, Chicago, IL 60610.